CATALINE

Caitlin Press Inc.
8100 Alderwood Road, Halfmoon Bay, BC V0N 1Y1
www.caitlin-press.com

Text and cover design by Vici Johnstone
Cover image A-02038 courtesy of the Royal BC Museum and Archives
Printed in Canada

Caitlin Press Inc. acknowledges financial support from the Government
of Canada and the Canada Council for the Arts, and the Province of
British Columbia through the British Columbia Arts Council and the
Book Publisher's Tax Credit.

Library and Archives Canada Cataloguing in Publication
Cataline : The life of BC's legendary packer / by Susan Smith-Josephy
with Irene Bjerky, C'eyxkn. Smith-Josephy, Susan, author. |
Bjerky C'eyxkn, Irene, 1960– author.
Includes bibliographical references.
Canadiana 20190233346 | ISBN 9781773860244 (softcover)
LCSH: Cataline, approximately 1829–1922. | LCSH: Muleteers—
British Columbia—Biography. | LCSH: Horsemen and horsewomen—
British Columbia—Biography. | LCSH: Pack transportation—British
Columbia—History. | LCSH: Frontier and pioneer life—British Colum-
bia. | LCSH: British Columbia—Biography. | LCGFT: Biographies.
LCC FC3822.1.C38 S65 2020 | DDC 971.1/02—dc23

CATALINE

The Life of
BC's Legendary Packer

SUSAN SMITH-JOSEPHY
with IRENE BJERKY

CAITLIN PRESS

Publisher's Note: We acknowledge that the use of the term "Indian" to refer to Canada's Indigenous Peoples is outdated, but is kept in direct quotes of historical documents throughout this text, to maintain the context of these documents.

CONTENTS

Oldest Packer in

While few photographs exist of Jean "Cataline" Caux, those that do show the weather-worn face and solid build of a man who fits the legends of the oldest and most famous of the gold rush packers of BC. Image 2003_30_4 courtesy of The Exploration Place

INTRODUCTION

by Irene Gail Bjerky,
C'eyxkn, Yale, BC

Cataline the packer—a fascinating yet elusive figure in BC history. 'Twas the stuff of myths and legends. He is sometimes referred to as North America's most famous packer, but some of the information was truly hard to find. So much speculation and conjecture.

Cataline is a famous, yet marginally shadowy figure in the historical records of our wonderful province. He's an enigma to me, and I spent years trying to track him through museums, books and newspaper accounts. Luckily, my career as a boilermaker took me along the pathways that he ran mule trains through for fifty-five years, and I was able to follow his trails. I have been chasing his character since 1973.

I heard tales of his honesty, his stamina and determination, and his various quirks of rubbing whisky into his hair and keeping order with a horseshoe. His deadly aim with a Mexican knife. His garbled mix of languages, his fair treatment of all races of men in his employ, his perfect memory for his accounts, and his custom of buying a brand-new white shirt on every trip. His habit of bathing naked in the snow or a fresh cold creek every morning. His ability to sleep outdoors with nothing but a tarp on the ground, and never wearing socks. It was Judge Begbie who helped to sponsor him as a Canadian citizen. The stories went on and on, each more interesting with every word I read.

I knew he was part of my family history; I know for certain he was the father of my great-grandmother's siblings and most likely the father of my own great-grandmother Clara. He chose to marry their Indigenous mother, Amelia, as a "country wife."

I have been given Amelia's Indigenous name of C'eyxkn. My great-grandmother Clara remembers having to run to the creek every day for her bath, then having to lash herself with cedar boughs. I have always wondered if this is where Cataline learned that practice of the daily bath ritual.

After at least eight years and several children later, he and Amelia parted ways, but he always took care of them with money and goods.

With the help of my research, Susan has written this book about my ancestor Jean Jacques "Cataline" Caux. Her continuing research is impeccable, and I learned many things from her manuscript that helped to fill out a lot of the facts. I learned that he had come from France with his brother Jean-Pierre in 1857 and that they had travelled and packed together for some years. I found out that they indeed had travelled to California, then came here to BC for the latest gold rush.

Another interesting thing that I discovered was that he was a packing partner with Joe Castillou, the father of Henry Castillou, "the Cowboy Judge of the Cariboo." It turned out that Joe Castillou, given the moniker "the Castillion," was born only seven miles (eleven kilometres) away from Cataline's town of Oloron-Sainte-Marie. They packed for James Alexander Teit, a famous ethnologist for the Boaz expeditions, who recorded a rapidly disappearing way of life for the Indigenous peoples of the BC Interior. Judge Henry and Teit both have excellently documented collections at the Nicola Valley Museum & Archives. Judge Henry recorded his recollections of these times, and of course everyone in historical circles knows of Teit's works on the Interior peoples.

I am so proud to be a part of Susan Smith-Josephy's book on Cataline and am so happy that she has included me as a contributor and fellow researcher.

Pack mules and horses loaded with provisions followed trails forged by the First Nations people and later used by the fur trading companies to travel between settlements in the rugged backcountry. Image WP2000-010-473 courtesy of the Prince Rupert City & Regional Archives

THE FRASER RIVER GOLD RUSH

In British Columbia's early days, pack trains of horses or mules were ubiquitous, and they played an extraordinarily important role in the province's development. Always at the forefront of settlement and industry, pack trains formed a lifeline for the explorers, traders, trappers, miners, settlers, merchants and builders of railways and telegraph lines. In the late 1850s, mules and horses carried provisions and equipment to the miners taking part in the Fraser River gold rush. In the 1860s, the miners forged their way north to the gold mines of the Cariboo and Barkerville, and they branched out to the Omineca, Stikine and Cassiar gold discoveries in the 1870s. Pack trains carried supplies to the workers building the Collins Overland Telegraph line in the 1870s and the Canadian Pacific Railway (CPR) in the 1880s, and by 1900, they were packing to the construction workers on the telegraph line to the Yukon and the Grand Trunk Pacific Railway to Prince Rupert.

Almost as important as the pack trains were the trails they followed, because these trails were not new. They had been created over the years by Indigenous peoples to travel between settlements in this rugged country. When the North West Company and, later, the Hudson's Bay Company arrived to establish fur-trading forts at the beginning of the nineteenth century, they saw the value of these trails and adapted and changed them to suit their needs. It was only after gold had been discovered that mule and horse pack trains were introduced, and the brigade's fur-trading trails were often used as pack trails. The packers also made their own trails if a more suitable route was found. In time, the pack trails became roads, and settlers and industries followed.

The most famous of all the men who ran the pack trains was Jean Caux, who would become known in British Columbia's history as the legendary packer "Cataline." His early life is largely undocumented, but it has been established that he was born in the little town of Oloron, in the department of Pyrénées-Atlantiques, in the Béarn region of southwestern France, just fifty kilometres from the border with Spain.[1] (In 1858, Oloron was combined with the neighbouring town of Sainte Marie, and they have since been known as Oloron-Sainte-Marie.) When he set off for America on the steamship *Mercury* in 1857, Caux was listed on the passenger manifest as being nineteen years of age, and his brother, Jean-Pierre, who accompanied him, was listed as twenty-one years old.[2] Canada's 1901 census records Jean Caux's birth date as December 20, 1838.[3]

The *Mercury* docked in New York on March 23, 1857, and although the brothers were identified as farmers on the manifest, they had apparently not come to North America to farm. Instead, they were headed for the other side of the continent, most likely in the hope of taking part in the California gold rush. How they got there from New York is not known, but a few years before his death, Jean Caux told the *Victoria Daily Times* that he had "crossed the ocean, gradually working his way west, and engaged in all manner of occupations until the [Fraser River] gold rush of 1858 brought him on the flood tide to this province."[4]

If the Caux brothers' original goal had been to take part in the California gold rush, they were too late. Since the mining frontier had already shifted to the Oregon Territory, they probably joined those trekking north on foot. It is possible they may have tried their hands at gold mining in Oregon, but as was the case in California, the rush there was virtually over by that time and the best claims had already been staked. Many of the miners, having heard rumours of gold on "Fraser's River," were already on the move again—either by ship or overland—into British territory north of the forty-ninth parallel. According to one source, the Caux brothers set off from Walla Walla in Washington Territory with a group of about sixty Mexican packers in charge of a train of four hundred horses and mules, arriving in Lytton in June 1858.[5] This enormous pack train was led by a man named Alvarez. Although this was not an unusual name among Mexicans, he might have been the A. Alvarez listed in the 1881 census for Cassiar as a packer, aged fifty-four years. Since there is no record of either of the Caux brothers taking out a miner's licence in British Columbia in 1858, it is possible they worked for Alvarez for the rest of that packing season. In fact, legend has it that it was a packer named Alvarez who sold them their first mules.

As farmers in the Béarn region of France, the brothers would have been accustomed to working with mules, because the breeding of Gascon (or Pyrénées) donkeys with Mérens or Castillonais horses to produce pack or riding mules has been a specialty of this area for centuries. These animals are particularly valued for their good temperament, their adaptability to all weather conditions and terrains and their absolute calm in difficult conditions. Thus, it is not surprising that many who knew Cataline in later years commented on his remarkable ability with mules and horses—he seemed to understand "their whims and vagaries as no other man could."[6] He was also helped by the fact that the mules the Mexican packers brought north were temperamentally much like the mules of Béarn because they were the progeny of strains of donkeys and horses originally raised in neighbouring Catalonia and imported to Mexico by the Spanish in the seventeenth century.

There are no photographs or contemporary accounts of the appearance of either Jean Caux or his brother during their earliest days in British Columbia, but numerous descriptions by those who knew Jean and photographs taken in later years make it plain that he was a handsome, well-built young man with curly black hair down to his shoulders, dark eyes and strong features. There is some question about his physique, however. All who knew him agreed that he was broad-shouldered, but few agreed on his height. Judge Henry Castillou described him as "not a very tall man, with way wide shoulders. My dad was the same size and build as he was, both from the same country of Béarn."[7] But William Manson, who served as the Indian Constable at Stoney Creek in the 1870s, saw him as "six feet or more, broad-shouldered, well-built."[8] Mrs. August Baker, née Suzie Elmore, who was born near Quesnel in 1866, remembered him as "a fair height, probably five feet ten inches or so." She owned a photograph of Cataline taken by J.P. Bome, a professional photographer in Ashcroft, and pointed out that "it makes him look as if he was a short man, but that must be because he was broad-shouldered."[9] Tall or short, he stood out among men because, as C.B. Bailey wrote, "when he moved on his moccasined feet, one felt the likeness to a giant panther—cautious, lithe, sure of himself—but never vindictive."[10]

According to Henry Castillou, when Jean Caux arrived in

British Columbia, "he spoke pure Béarnese and had no educa-
tion whatsoever. It was only the educated man in the kingdom of
Béarn that spoke much French."[11] But the Canadian census of
1891, taken thirty years after his arrival in BC, indicated he could
read and write, and the 1901 census reported that he could not
only speak French but could read, write and speak English as well.
This may have been an exaggeration, since throughout his life he
relied on merchants and friends to write his business correspondence, only signing his name to these documents in a scrawled
hand. James Brown, who was born near Lillooet and spent his
early life in Dog Creek, where he published a newspaper called
The Rural Backwoodsman, told an interviewer in 1930 that he had
known Cataline in the 1880s and that

> the first time I saw him I remember he wanted me
> to write some letters for him. He had a pleasant
> voice, low in tone in ordinary conversation, and
> you could tell he was a foreigner by his accent,
> but when he had to he could roar like a bull
> at his packers and curse them. He sang a good
> deal while riding along and was fond of playing
> the fiddle.[12]

When the Caux brothers arrived in British Columbia in
1858, the colony was in unprecedented turmoil. Since the end of
the eighteenth century, the men of the Hudson's Bay Company,
which had enjoyed a monopoly on trade west of the Rockies and
north of the forty-ninth parallel, had endeavoured to make their
relationship with the Indigenous population as peaceful as possible
since they numbered only a few hundred compared to an estimated 100,000 Indigenous people. Although hostile incidents had

occurred from time to time, interactions remained mostly harmonious as they developed trading partnerships—primarily the exchange of manufactured goods for furs—that were beneficial to both parties. But in the 1850s, the company had begun buying gold dust from the Yale and Nlaka'pamux people on the Fraser and Thompson Rivers, being careful to keep the trade quiet to avoid an influx of miners from the California goldfields. Then, in spite of the company's caution, in the summer of 1857 a group of American miners turned up where the Thompson River meets the Fraser. Their arrival totally disrupted the status quo, because the gold these men were seeking lay in the same rivers that provided the salmon that had allowed the rich West Coast Indigenous cultures to develop.

That December, as the influx of miners continued to grow, James Douglas, governor of the crown colony of Vancouver Island, responded by announcing the extension of colonial authority over the entire mainland from the forty-ninth parallel northward. He followed this up by declaring Victoria the only legal access point to the goldfields and stationing a gunboat at the mouth of the Fraser River to collect a licence fee of ten shillings (or $2.50 in American funds) from all miners entering the colony. This action gave him temporary control of the gold rush, because most of the miners in the initial wave were coming north from San Francisco by ship. Landing in Victoria, they boarded one of the steamers that carried passengers and freight from the "outside" across Georgia Strait to New Westminster, where they loaded up with supplies, and took it up the Fraser to the head of navigation at Yale. The little settlement there already boasted an Anglican church, a schoolhouse, a jail and a number of stores, hotels and blacksmith shops. Commercial freighting and forwarding, which

In 1858, the Hudson's Bay Company reopened their fort at Yale, which quickly became the main supply depot for miners and packers heading north. After the gold rush, Front Street's Branch Hotel would become a meeting place of the Confederation League in the 1860s. Image A-03615 courtesy of the Royal BC Museum and Archives

would become the town's leading industry, was still in its infancy.

In early May 1858, Douglas learned that miners were also crossing the border into the colony on overland trails from Washington Territory with all their supplies on their backs, and he passed an order-in-council declaring that in future any goods not imported through Victoria would be confiscated; this act ensured that the money the miners brought into the colony would stay in the colony. For Victoria, this meant that most miners arriving by boat would now kit themselves out with clothing, boots, picks, pans and basic foodstuffs bought from the local merchants, especially the Hudson's Bay Company. Those arriving overland were forced to purchase their supplies at the Hudson's Bay Company's newly reopened fort at Yale (which had been closed since 1849). This fort quickly became the main supply depot for individual miners as well as for the packers carrying goods north.

⚬⚬

The first major strike of the Fraser River gold rush occurred in the early months of 1858 at Hill's Bar, a low sand and gravel bank on the east side of the river just downstream from Yale. The bar was just forty metres long, but this bit of gold-laden shoreline drew miners by the hundreds. In the Halq'emélem language, the place was called Hemhemethqw, meaning "a good place to make sockeye salmon oil," and thus friction soon developed between the miners and the Indigenous people. Major trouble erupted later that spring when miners who had entered the colony via the Okanagan brigade trail ambushed and killed a group of Indigenous people and razed several villages. But it was only when miners began building cabins on the traditional territories of the Nlaka'pamux or Thompson River people that the Indigenous people retaliated by blockading the Fraser River at Big Canyon to prevent the interlopers from going upriver past that point. And after the alleged rape of a Nlaka'pamux woman at Kanaka Bar, they sent the headless bodies of two French miners floating downstream.

As they had done in Oregon, the miners reacted by organizing militia companies, and on August 14, two armed companies marched north to confront the Nlaka'pamux. The Whatcom Company, under the command of a Captain Graham, was composed of men determined to exterminate the Indigenous people as they had done in Oregon so they could get on with gold mining. Instead they exterminated themselves in a nighttime gun battle in which they mistakenly believed they were being attacked and shot each other. The Pike Guards, led by "Captain" Harry M. Snyder, confronted the Indigenous people at the Forks, soon to be known as Lytton, where hundreds of warriors and twenty-seven chiefs from the Nlaka'pamux, Secwépemc, Nicola, Okanagan and other Indigenous peoples had gathered. Fortunately, before the Pike Guards arrived, a chief and great orator named CexpentlEm (Spintlum) had made an eloquent speech that convinced the assembly to pursue peace with the miners. Thus, when Snyder presented an ultimatum of either accepting peace or being driven from their lands, the Indigenous people agreed to the peace treaty he had prepared.

Meanwhile, Douglas's authority on the mainland had been legitimized by the Colonial Office in London, which officially established the mainland as the Crown Colony of British Columbia, picked the Hudson's Bay Company's Fort Langley as its capital and named Douglas governor. London had also sent out Colonel Richard Clement Moody at the head of a detachment of Royal Engineers to build roads and other infrastructure and keep the peace. By the time the Royal Engineers arrived, the trickle of miners coming from the south had become a flood; official records indicate that just over 15,000 would-be miners came into the port of Victoria between April and August 1858.[13] Many more were arriving overland, crossing the border on trails used for centuries by Indigenous peoples, and in the end, about one-third of the approximately 90,000 men (and women) who had sought their fortunes in California had made their way north, either by sea or overland, to seek gold on the Fraser River. They were joined by Chinese, Australians, Mexicans, Europeans and people from Upper and Lower Canada.

Those miners who had come too late to stake claims at Hill's Bar moved upriver eleven miles (nineteen kilometres) past Yale to Spuzzum, and from there, another eleven miles (nineteen kilometres) to Boston Bar. Both of these bars, however, are within the Fraser Canyon with its rocky cliffs and roaring torrents, which Matthew Baillie Begbie, the Cambridge-educated lawyer Douglas chose as judge for the new colony, would later describe as "utterly impassable for any animal except man, goat or dog."[14] Undeterred by the dangers, the miners devised a complicated and treacherous system of rope holds and flimsy scaffolding or scrabbled among the boulders rising out of the rushing waters at the bottom of the canyon, but it was obvious that this route was impractical and far too dangerous for the mass of men determined to venture upriver. In his report to London, Governor Douglas expressed his concern:

> Many accidents have happened in the dangerous rapids of that river, a great number of canoes having been slashed to pieces and their cargoes swept away by the impetuous stream, while some of the ill-fated adventurers who occupied them may have been swept away into eternity.[15]

His solution was typical of his practicality: by offering two square meals a day, he was able to recruit miners to clear an old trail on the west side of the river that bypassed some of the most treacherous parts of the canyon. This trail, which had been previously used by both First Nations people and fur traders, ended at Spuzzum, where in September 1858, Frank Way, who had opened a roadhouse at that point on the river, received a permit from the government to install a cable ferry. He charged a toll that he had to share with the government, and he had no regular schedule and was sometimes absent for days while he went fishing or hunting.[16] After the miners crossed to the east side of the river, they could follow a Hudson's Bay Company brigade trail for another six miles (ten kilometres) to Chapman's Bar. Entrepreneurs also installed ferries on the Fraser River near Lytton and on the Thompson River approximately a mile (1.6 kilometres) below the mouth of the Nicola River.

When this new route became bottlenecked with the massive volume of miners arriving, Douglas was reminded of a trail that had been vetted thirty years earlier by the Hudson's Bay Company. It began at the north end of Harrison Lake and followed the Lillooet River, then turned northwest to Anderson Lake, with a portage to Seton Lake before ending at Lillooet, which sits on the eastern edge of the Coast Mountains. The Royal Engineers surveyed it, then supervised its construction by private contractors who hired miners to do the pick-and-shovel work for £5 apiece, payable after the road reached Lillooet. The contractors were then given the right to collect tolls on their portions of the road, which they did until 1871, when British Columbia joined Confederation. After completion of the new trail, which became known as the Douglas Road, a steamer called the *Lady of the Lake* began carrying miners to Port Douglas at the head of Harrison Lake; smaller steamboats provided transport on both Anderson and Seton Lakes. In the next few years, 20,000 to 30,000 miners scrambled over this Lakes Route to Lillooet, which in a short time peaked at a population of 16,000.[17]

After word reached Victoria about the conflict in the Fraser Canyon, Governor Douglas set out with a force of twenty Royal Marines and fifteen Royal Engineers, arriving in Yale on

Port Douglas, located at the head of Harrison Lake, was one of the largest settlements in British Columbia during the Fraser Canyon gold rush. Image A-03519 courtesy of the Royal BC Museum and Archives

September 13. Knowing he must protect the Crown's fragile coalition with Indigenous people because he would need them if the Americans tried to take over his new colonies, he reprimanded the miners vigorously for ignoring British authority and was given their assurances that they would follow British law in the future. Afterwards he met with the Nlaka'pamux chiefs and guaranteed them reserve lands in the Fraser Canyon and then ordered the prohibition of alcohol sales to all Indigenous people. With peace restored, he designated townsites for Hope and Yale, chose justices of the peace for Hill's Bar and Yale from among the more educated miners, appointed five constables for the area, and was back in Victoria on September 20.

Lillooet was originally known as Cayoosh Flat but was renamed for the Líl'wat, the Interior Salish people who live in the area. It was designated Mile 0 on the first road to the Cariboo but lost that designation after the Royal Engineers completed the Cariboo Road to Barkerville in 1865. In the mid-1880s, Chinese miners found gold on lower Cayoosh Creek, and a decade later the single largest deposit of gold ever found in BC was discovered in the nearby valley of the Bridge River. Image A-09064 courtesy of the Royal BC Museum and Archives

Douglas's actions did not put an end to the violence in the goldfields, although the next rounds did not involve Indigenous people. Instead, it was a clash among factions of the California miners, who had brought their political conflicts north with them. By the end of 1858, Hill's Bar was controlled by Edward "Ned"

McGowan, a discredited politician and judge from San Francisco, along with a group of gamblers, thugs and thieves who had been associated with him in California's Law and Order Party. At the same time, Yale was dominated by members of the notorious Vigilance Committee that had ruled San Francisco by summary executions of suspected criminals.

What came to be known as Ned McGowan's War began at a Christmas 1858 dance and party in Yale at which two miners from Hill's Bar objected to the attendance of Isaac Dixon, Yale's black American barber. (Another version of this story places the incident in Dixon's barber shop.) After one of the miners assaulted him, Dixon laid a complaint with Yale's justice of the peace, Peter Whannell, and was promptly placed in "protective custody." Then, encouraged by the men of the Vigilance Committee, Whannell issued a warrant for the arrest of the alleged perpetrator and ordered that the warrant be served in Hill's Bar. Meanwhile, George Perrier, the justice of the peace for Hill's Bar, was also investigating the case and, urged on by McGowan, sent his constable, Henry Hickson, to Yale to pick up Dixon and bring him to Hill's Bar for interrogation. Hickson, noting that Whannell's constable had failed to arrest the perpetrator, took the man into custody himself and proceeded with him to Yale. In his attempt to serve Perrier's warrant for the arrest of Dixon, he interrupted Whannell's court, was charged with contempt of court and found himself sharing a cell with both the perpetrator and the victim of the original crime.

Perrier's response was to swear in special constables—one of them Ned McGowan—and give them instructions to proceed to Yale and there secure the persons of his constable and the perpetrator of the assault as well as Magistrate Whannell himself because

Perrier now accused him of contempt of *his* court. The posse, led by McGowan and a man named Kelly, proceeded upriver by boat with an American flag flying and threw open Yale's jailhouse. After Whannell, who was brought before Perrier and fined fifty dollars, was allowed to return to Yale, he played on Governor Douglas's fear of American intentions by sending word to him that

> the town and district are in a state bordering on anarchy. My own and the lives of the citizens are in imminent peril.... An effective blow must at once be struck on the operations of these outlaws, else I tremble for the welfare of the colony.[18]

Whannell's letter brought Colonel Richard Clement Moody and his Royal Engineers, accompanied by Justice Matthew Baillie Begbie, upriver to Yale, where the presence of Moody and his troops had an immediate calming effect. Begbie held court, and on hearing the long list of charges and countercharges, he dismissed both magistrates from their posts and fined McGowan for assault. The war was now over. The next day being Sunday, Colonel Moody held divine service for a congregation of thirty or forty miners.

Begbie was already forty years old when he arrived in the colony with a mandate to establish law and order. He did so by taking the law to the people in the form of the traditional British system of circuit courts known as assizes, always appearing in his makeshift courtrooms dressed in full regalia in order to impress both miscreants and the general public with the seriousness of the proceedings. His authority ultimately perpetuated a legacy of discrimination and betrayal for the Indigenous community.

Jean Caux, who met Begbie during these times of turmoil in the Yale area, was evidently one of those who was thoroughly impressed by the judge. Later in life he enjoyed telling the story of their first encounter. According to his friend Sperry Cline, the story went something like this:

> Judge Begbie was coming up the river dispensing justice in the various camps and was not always welcomed by the lawless element. Feeling was running high, and opinion about submitting to authority was about evenly divided. The newly arrived packers were asked which side they would support. Cataline coolly drew a long Mexican knife from his boot and answered, "I standa by judge!" As he had a considerable number of stalwart packers in support, his decision was not disputed.[19]

However, this very public stand in favour of Begbie and British law may have been the cause of Jean Caux's run-in with a couple of thieves a short time later. That event, as retold years later to Ernest Thoreson, began:

> I was packing for some miners out of Yale…. The trip lasted 27 days into southeastern BC [probably via the Dewdney Trail to Rock Creek]. I returned to Yale and put my mules in a corral near the river. That evening before going to bed I decided to go down and see if my mules were well supplied with hay. On my way back two men jumped me, armed with knives. I threw up my left arm to ward off the knife[;]

at the same time I hit him in the jaw with my right fist and with a swift kick caught the other robber in the stomach. I grabbed the two of them by the collar and dragged them up to the jail. The next morning these two men were aboard a steamer heading downriver. They were in bad shape. Ned McGowan, [that] bad man from California, ruled the roost of Yale in the early days and these two robbers were no doubt members of his gang. Yale was tough and there were killings most every day.

According to Thoreson, Cataline had laughed and added, "I don't think those hombres enjoyed a meal for quite some time."[20]

⚬══⚬

As was the case in California and Oregon, only a very few of the many thousands who came looking for gold on the Fraser River found the riches they were seeking, and within months of arriving, many went home broke. Others remained for years, following the river and its tributaries farther and farther north, convinced they would find their fortunes beyond the next bend. Most of them never did. However, the smarter ones among them realized there was a better way to make a fortune in British Columbia than looking for gold. These were the entrepreneurs who put aside their picks and shovels to install ferries and bridges, build roadhouses and saloons, barber and blacksmithing shops, laundries and general stores. But the most enterprising of them all became packers, because the entire economy depended on the goods they carried, and they had Governor Douglas and his improved roads and trails to thank for much of their success.

With the discovery of gold on the Fraser and the resulting improvement in the sale of provisions at the Hudson's Bay Company's trading posts, that company began buying horses to establish its own pack trains to bring goods north from Yale, but it was also happy to contract work out to the independent Mexican packers who had suddenly arrived in the colony with their mule trains. Most of these men had originated in the Sonora region of Mexico, where they had been miners, but when they moved north in 1848 to take part in the California gold rush, they had found it more profitable to use their pack animals to carry provisions from San Francisco to the miners in the goldfields on the western slopes of the Sierras. While many had returned to Mexico after the California gold rush ended in 1855, some had moved north into Oregon Territory where, as well as provisioning miners, they had packed supplies for the volunteer militias battling the Indigenous people in the bloody Rogue River Wars. By June 1856, those battles were over, but the Oregon gold rush was also winding down. Fortunately, confirmation of gold discoveries on the Fraser River reached them in the spring of 1858, and soon they and their pack trains were on the move north again via the Hudson's Bay Company's Okanagan Brigade Trail.

These Mexican pack-train veterans dominated the trade in the new colony for the next twenty years because of their skill and experience, but also because they had come into this rugged country with mules, which they preferred to horses because they were sure-footed, sturdier and had flatter backs than horses and could carry up to 500 pounds (227 kilograms) each, almost twice as much as a horse could carry. The Mexicans' dominance also meant that the packing traditions and Spanish terminology they used became standard for the profession in British Columbia until well into the twentieth century. And they were respected because they were "absolute experts" at their trade, according to early Hazelton resident Alan Benson, who had watched the packing process when he was young.

> Those [animals] carried the same pack every day. They're caught up about two in the morning and they're packed before 3 o'clock—before the flies get to the mules and make them fussy… and the *corregidor* gives the word. He's the boss of the show and the *segundo* comes under him. He gives the orders to the men. They ring a bell and the mules and horses come into their positions… like a cow to its stall, without fail.

Saddling up began with placing three layers of blankets over an animal's back before adding the pack saddle or *aparejo*, which was designed to prevent the load rubbing on the animal's back. It consisted of two large, square horsehide panniers stuffed with straw, grass or moss and connected by a flat section of leather. A broad leather crupper (a strap) led from the back edge of these sacks and passed under the tail, and a *latigo* or cinch strap went from one sack to the other under the animal's belly. The actual packing of the cargo began with hoisting large boxes or sacked goods of equal weight onto either side of the *aparejo*, tying them in place with a sling rope, then piling the remaining items on top. The whole pack was then secured with fifty or sixty feet (fifteen to eighteen metres) of rope.[21] Benson recalled that

> then they throw the diamond [hitch] on, a two-man diamond, and if it's a hard pack to hold or a round-backed horse, they might throw an extra

> diamond or even three diamonds on there. They
> tighten three times—say, a half-mile from camp,
> then another mile—and then they're away. They
> never touch a pack after that for five hours.[22]

If the packs were not fastened securely, they would slip forward on the downhill trails and slip back again on the uphills, resulting in painful sores on the animals' backs. As soon as all the mules were loaded, the cook would climb onto his horse and lead the bell mare—so-called because it wore a large cowbell around its neck—out of camp with the whole train following in single file. The train master or *cargador* checked the animals one by one as they passed him to make sure they were in good health, the equipment in good repair and the cargo correctly packed. By eleven o'clock in the morning, the mule train would stop at a place where there was sufficient pasture and water for the animals, their packs would be removed, and the train would camp for the day.

One of the few existing eyewitness accounts of a trip with a pack train in these very early pioneer days in British Columbia was made by trader Frank Sylvester, who told his story to the Victoria Board of Trade in 1907 or 1908, nearly fifty years after the event. In those early gold rush days, he had set himself up with a little store in Lillooet, but in the spring of 1860, when he had "tired of the advance of civilization" around him, he set off to try his luck selling to miners and ranchers farther north.

> So in the early part of the year, I purchased
> a new stock of goods, went in with Snyder &
> Linny in their pack train, and started for Fort
> Alexander [Alexandria], at that time the head
> of mule navigation on the Fraser. I left Lillooet

on March 12 and we were the second train of the year to leave.... Our train consisted of 42 mules, none carrying less than 300 pounds [136 kilograms], and a few as high as 400 pounds [181 kilograms].... The rule of pack trains was two men to every ten mules, and we had consequently eight Mexicans as packers, besides the Indian who rode ahead and led the bell mare.... These animals come for two purposes: while travelling, [the bell mare carries] the precious "kitchen," usually two boxes containing all the camp silver-ware, namely the tin cups, tin plates and iron spoons. We had no knives and forks as forks were not needed... as the menu consisted daily of bacon & beans.... All the men of the train rode mules or horses, but we had about 20 miners who were going north with us who walked the entire way, although we packed their blankets, etc., on top of one pack, free.

When we left Lillooet, the Fraser was still frozen over solid, and we crossed the river on the ice with the loaded train. We left in the early morning but only went as far as the Fountain. Seven miles [eleven kilometres] the first day, just so as to get our packs and everything in perfect order before getting away too far. The trail to the Fountain, where Lorenzo had his place, follows the bank of the Fraser right along and was pretty good.... The next day we struck in to the right, leaving the river, so as to go around back of Pavilion Mountain, and managed to get to what was called Reynolds Ranch, which was about a 16-mile [26-kilometre] drive. I did not see much sign of any ranch, but everything was froze up.

A pack train, as a rule, does not travel more than 15 miles [24 kilometres] per day with loaded animals, as they travel very slowly—in fact, they just walk. The road all the way to Reynolds Ranch was very bad indeed, being full of deep ravines, sharp pitches and slides, and as the ground was pretty well covered with hard snow and ice, especially on the side hills where the sun could not penetrate, we had lots of trouble all day long. At Reynolds Ranch we had to lay over for two days to cut steps in the ice on the face of a bad cliff or bluff, so that we could get around a little lake.... Here is where the kind help of our miner friends came in, as they un-slung their picks and shovels and helped out nicely to cut the steps for the trail. The weather was nice, not snowing, clear but intensely cold—I would judge at least 40 [degrees Fahrenheit] below.

From here we passed, heading I think almost northeast, by Marble Canyon and Hat Creek and then on to the Bonaparte River. We were now on the old Brigade Trail.... The country we had been travelling along up till here was very rough and broken, but the scenery changed greatly at the [Bonaparte]. Here we came into nice rolling prairie land with lots of fine bunch grass, although of course, most of it as yet was covered with snow. We crossed and re-crossed the Bonaparte three times, once at the Round mound and once each at the first and second crossing ford, always fording the stream, but the fords were well known. We continued on by Green Lake, a fine sheet of water, on which we saw lots of wild geese and ducks, past the Deep Correll and then on the Bridge Creek, as it is now called. Then on past Lake La Hache to Williams Lake, 40 miles [64 kilometres] from Fort Alexander. On this travel we had [to] go through what was called Green Timber, a drive of 25 miles [40 kilometres] in one day as there was no feed until we got through, and it was very bad travelling....

The occupation of a packer was a wild, free and exciting one. Going up with a loaded train, it was certainly very, very, hard work indeed. Lifting daily the heavy packs, riding and mounting and dismounting perhaps 50 times a day, hunting up the mules in the cold, dark early morning in the long wet grass, living on the very rudest of fare, sleeping on the bare ground. But once the cargo had been delivered and the mules all unloaded, the return trip was a real picnic. Empty animals travel much faster than when loaded. Returning, we would often travel 25 miles [40 kilometres] a day, keeping the mules on a trot on good ground. Then there was nothing to do during the day's ride but jog along on your mule or horse, smoke your pipe or cigarette and spin yarns.

A loaded pack train wending its way along a smooth, nice, rolling prairie is really a most picturesque scene. There is first the Indian riding ahead, and leading the bell mare or bell horse. Then comes the long string of loaded animals strung out almost in single file, each mule grunting heavily as they walk along as though he were in pain. Behind came the bunch of Mexican or white riders, each with his leather leggings, heavy spurs and huge saddles, and then there was the shouts and calls to the mules, to keep them moving along until suddenly two horsemen would dash out, single out some mule whose load their helpful eye told them was not properly balanced or perhaps had shifted, jump from their saddles, throw their bridle reins over their horse's head, catch the mule required, "blind" him, quickly adjust the load, mount again in an instant and be away.... [But] riding horsemen, no matter how romantic, on a very hot summer day over a prairie behind a loaded train, you could hardly see from the dust. When camp was reached, you could not tell the Mexican from the white, all were covered with dust and perspiration....[23]

This, then, was the life to which the Caux brothers had committed themselves, but they were more comfortable in it than most because they probably spoke enough Spanish to get along easily with the Mexicans they rode with. Jean Caux's closest known friendship in these early years was Jesus Garcia, who had been born in Hermosillo, Mexico, in 1846, and who had moved to the United States when he was seventeen to pack to the silver mines. Like many of the Mexican packers who came to British Columbia, Garcia married an Indigenous woman, Qwayntko (also known as Mary), whose father was Humsinna, a Nlaka'pamux chief from the Spuzzum area.

THE CARIBOO GOLD RUSH

There was very little work for packers in the winter months when the trails were snowed in. In February 1859, the Caux brothers went to Lytton, which had become the government centre for the Nicola and Okanagan Valleys and everything to the north. Lytton boasted a saloon, a courthouse, an express office and numerous businesses in the early 1860s. H.M. Ball was the stipendiary magistrate, coroner, collector of revenue and gold commissioner, while Captain O. Travaillot supervised the revenue office. Between them they ensured that miners were licensed, duties were paid, road tolls collected and illegal liquor kept out of the country.

The Caux brothers took out $5 miner's licences in 1859—apparently their first in British Columbia since there is no previous record of licences issued to them. Jean Caux's licence number was 106, his brother's 197,[24] but it is not known whether they actually worked as miners that year.

At this time, things were changing in the colony's gold rush country. The vast crowds of miners had thinned out, because many of the Americans had become convinced the Fraser River's gold had been a hoax. Now the diggings were primarily the focus of men and women from eastern Canada, Britain and China, and

In the late 1850s, Lytton was the government centre for the Nicola and Okanagan Valleys, dealing with everything from miners' licences to liquor confiscation. It
was here that the Caux brothers procured their first-known miner licences for
$5 each in 1859. Image G-00782 courtesy of the Royal BC Museum and Archives

even before the snows melted that year, most of them were push-
ing north, investigating every river and stream along the way. It
was one of the remaining Americans, however, who established
the next major claim. In the spring of 1859, Peter Curran Dunlevy and four friends were panning for gold at the confluence of
the Fraser and Chilcotin Rivers when an Indigenous man offered
to guide them to a stream where there was "gold like beans." He
took them to Little Horsefly Creek, northeast of Williams Lake,
and suddenly the colony's gold rush was on again.

The next important strike occurred in the spring of 1860 on
Keithley Creek, forty-five miles (seventy-three kilometres) east of
Quesnel, but in the middle of the following winter, word leaked

out that an even better strike had been made on the far side of Yank's Peak at Antler Creek, and miners who had been settled for the winter at Keithley Creek and Quesnel Forks began snowshoeing towards Antler. When Philip Henry Nind, assistant gold commissioner, arrived at Antler Creek in early March 1861, he found the four original claimants living in the tiny cabin they had built there, while the other hopefuls had carved out caves in the deep snow.[25] By July of that year, 1200 miners were at work on Antler Creek; by September, their town boasted sixty houses, ten saloons, seven general stores, two blacksmiths, a sawmill, a shoemaker, a butcher shop and even a racecourse with horses imported from England.[26]

THREE YEARS IN CARIBOO

In 1862, Jo Lindley, who had spent three years as a packer in British Columbia, published a book in San Francisco entitled *Three Years in Cariboo: Being the Experience and Observations of a Packer, What I Saw and Know of the Country; Its Traveled Routes, Distances, Villages, Mines, Trade and Prospects with Distances, Notes and Facts*. After providing pages of detailed notes on the various routes available and expounding on the difficulties awaiting those intent on joining the Cariboo gold rush, he warned his readers that

> too many persons go to Cariboo with the entirely mistaken notions of the difficulties to be encountered; they will not believe one-half that is told them of the fatigues of the journey or the labor necessary to open out successfully a paying claim; they base their calculations too much upon previous experience in California

or elsewhere, which will not apply to the gold fields of Cariboo. No man going there should expect to make much more than expenses the first season unless he is able to buy into a good paying claim at once. The cost of prospecting for a claim is often-times enormous, on account of the high price of provisions and supplies of every kind. You cannot take a mule, pack him with "grub," tools and blankets, and start off on a two or three weeks' prospecting tour, as in California. The extreme roughness of the hill lands and quagmire condition of the low country absolutely forbid it. A great deal of the country is so densely timbered that even grass cannot grow in sufficient abundance to maintain animals, at the same time that it presents an almost impenetrable barrier to progress.

But even these obstacles might be in a measure overcome and the mines more rapidly developed but for the shortness of the season. Four months is the longest term of surface mining that can be hoped for, and during that short period a great deal of the time drenching rains are falling and flooding everything around you—mining claim, camping grounds, tents—nothing escapes the constant soaking; so that if you succeed against all these drawbacks in hunting up, prospecting and fairly opening out a good claim ready for a second season's successful operations, you may consider yourself fortunate.[27]

Meanwhile, in order to finance further road and trail construction, back in March 1860 Governor Douglas had imposed a toll of one pound sterling on "every pack horse, mule or other quadruped leaving Port Douglas or Yale for the purpose of carrying a load or burden towards the mining regions beyond." The fine for those caught evading the toll collector was triple the toll.

Douglas's move turned out to be an effective money-raiser, and in a little over a year, the government had collected enough funds to provide a grant of $2000 to improve the rough trail the miners had created beyond 150 Mile House that passed close to Quesnel Forks at the confluence of the Cariboo and Quesnel Rivers, then headed northeast to Keithley Creek and over Yank's Peak to Antler. With this encouragement from the government, the merchants at Quesnel Forks and Keithley Creek donated another $800, and the new trail was finished by midsummer. When gold strikes were subsequently made on Grouse, Williams and Lightning Creeks, the miners and packers extended the trail again on their own initiative, and after Billy Barker's discovery of gold on Williams Creek the following August, they extended it yet again. Since it would be used by sleighs in winter, they made it wider than the usual mule and horse pack trails.

⟜

The town of Barkerville sprang up next to Billy Barker's claim. At first, it was just a jumble of log and false-fronted stores, hotels, restaurants, saloons, dance halls and brothels perched on posts along a single muddy street. It burned to the ground in September 1868, but within six weeks, it had been rebuilt in a more orderly fashion along a wider street.

For the next four years this trail was well-used by thousands of miners and pack trains as well as by herds of dairy cows and

In order to finance the continued construction of roads and trails, tolls of £1 sterling (the equivalent of over $200 CAD today) were collected for each pack horse, mule or any other animal used for the purpose of carrying supplies north. Image WP2000-010-482 courtesy of the Prince Rupert City & Regional Archives

the cattle and sheep being driven to the slaughterhouse established at Richfield. But while the trail may have been passable when first established, whenever it rained, it became a quagmire. In early spring, the mud was covered with a slick layer of ice, and when the mud dried out in summer, each footfall kicked up so much dust that by the end of the day it had seeped into every crack and crevasse of harness and clothing; in winter, the trail was covered by as much as ten feet (three metres) of snow.

Although the Caux brothers were probably employed by other packers during the early years of this new gold rush, they were soon acting as entrepreneurs in their own right, demonstrated by the fact that on September 20, 1862, Jean Caux took out trading licence #682 for a period of three months. From the tolls listed in the Toll and Duty Record books for fall that year, it is clear as well that they had begun to invest in pack animals of their own. They seem to have started with just one animal, which was probably a horse, not a mule, given the weight of the load it carried; in an entry for October 10, 1862, its toll weight was 225 pounds (102 kilograms), and on November 12, 1862, just 275 pounds (125 kilograms). A year later on October 22, 1863, J. Caux paid a toll for four animals, again most likely horses since their pack load had a total weight of only 994 pounds (450 kilograms).[28]

While the brothers would no doubt have preferred mules, since they had become accustomed to working with them back home, in British Columbia mules were far more expensive than horses because they were not bred in BC and had to be imported from the southern United States or Mexico. In 1860, two mule trains, one composed of thirty-four mules, the other thirty-two, each with a bell mare, had been brought north from Washington Territory for sale; one train sold for $5150, the other for $4750, or about $150 a head. Prices were often higher for a single mule in good condition.[29] In addition, purchasing mules, their harnesses and pack saddles required cash, which the brothers obviously did not have, or taking out a loan or chattel mortgage.

Pack trains in British Columbia at this time ranged in size from just a few animals to thirty or more, but most packers aimed for trains of about twenty-five animals because this number was most efficient for local road and trail conditions and could travel with as few as four packers. The cost of running a successful pack train, however, was still high. The men who worked the trains had to be paid well because it was such specialized work; in the early 1860s, they received about $100 a month plus expenses and food, while a train master could make as much as $150 a month. (By the end of the century, this had slipped to $50 for crew and $100 for the train master.) In exchange, they worked long days and had to be ready for any eventuality or emergency—trails washed out, relentless rain, broiling sun, unexpected snowstorms, an injured, ill or strayed animal, and cargo damaged or lost. Although the train stopped at many of the roadhouses along the way, the packers themselves always slept outside—even in rain or snow—in order to oversee their animals. Packing also required the men to be away from home for at least six months of the year, so it was devastating for family life. In his old age, James Watt, who had been a veteran train master, recalled that

> the packers certainly earned their money.… The packers I worked among were, take them all in all, a rough, lawless and profane bunch of men, but they were brave, hardy and extremely loyal and trustworthy towards their employers. [30]

The key to a packer's success was speed and reliability, but pack animals moved so slowly—usually 8 to 10 miles (13 to 16 kilometres) per day—that it took more than a month for a pack train that had loaded up in Yale to reach the heart of the Cariboo goldfields 350 miles (570 kilometres) away. There were delays where downed trees blocked the trail or where detours around slides or washouts were necessary, and encounters with outfits coming from the opposite direction would bring the whole train to a standstill. Packing overweight or unwieldy items, like the billiard tables and pianos that were indispensable for the operation of saloons, slowed the entire train down; the son of one early packer recalled the difficulties his father had transporting four billiard tables from the Fountain to Barkerville—although he earned $4000 for taking on the job. And the pack train would move even more slowly when it was carrying special items such as the boiler and engine that were transported to the upper Fraser River for the first steamer to be launched there in 1862 or the 667-pound (302.5-kilogram) gold stamp mill that had to be transported a hundred miles (160 kilometres) for the government gold commissioner.

Most cargoes were fairly routine, however, and consisted of nonperishable staples such as bacon, flour, rice, sugar, salt, beans, coffee, tea, tobacco and whisky, plus heavy woollen jackets and trousers, "oilskins" and rubber boots, because these items wore out quickly in the cold and wet working conditions the miners endured. The pack trains also carried pickaxes and shovels that the miners required to sink their shafts to reach bedrock, plus windows, stoves, nails, saws, hammers and other building tools needed to construct the cabins, stores, saloons and gaming establishments that grew up wherever there was a successful gold strike, all built of rough-cut lumber. Once these communities were established, the packers added luxury goods such as champagne and canned and bottled comestibles to their loads, since successful miners seldom hoarded their newly found wealth. For the most part, goods were consigned by a third party and destined for a particular store or trading post, although at least one of the animals in each train carried food supplies used directly by the pack crew, while several more carried goods that the train master or *cargador* had invested in—goods that he intended to sell, usually at a high markup, to miners, ranchers or Indigenous people along the way.

Miners were charged very high prices for basic necessities. S.G. Hathaway, a veteran of the California gold rush, wrote in his diary on August 6, 1862:

> Got into the new town of Van Winkle on Lightning Creek on Saturday July 18. Provisions dear and scarce. Flour $1.25 a pound, tea $3, salt $5 for a 3-pound bag, nails $3 a pound & hardly any to be had. My partners growled all the way up because I thought best to bring some nails along—they wish now we had brought all nails! Sold Billy Mule at once for $140 & found on dividing our goods that I had provisions enough to last me 5 or 6 weeks.... My partners got discouraged in a day or two & went off, & I expect they are out of Cariboo by this time.[31]

A dollar in 1862 was the equivalent of approximately sixteen dollars today.

A large part of the price miners were charged for goods in the goldfields was due to the cost of freighting. In her book *The West Beyond the West*, historian Jean Barman explains that

> a bag of flour worth $16 in Whatcom sold for $25 at Fort Langley, $36 at Fort Hope and $100 at the most distant diggings. While it cost just over $20 to dispatch a ton of freight from London to Victoria, the charge from Victoria to the farthest reach of the gold fields surpassed $200 by 1859.[32]

In April 1859, the *Times* correspondent in British Columbia estimated that

> while it cost just over 1¢ per lb to carry goods from London to Victoria, the cost of moving goods from Victoria to the gold mines was about eleven times greater (11.6¢).... In July 1862, at the very height of the Cariboo gold rush, the cost of freighting goods from either Lillooet or Yale to the gold fields reached as high as 65¢ per pound.[33]

The prices that packers charged also fluctuated according to the number of pack animals available and the number of general stores, trading posts, saloons and hotels vying for their services. For example, since spring was late to arrive in 1862, the pack trains were late leaving for the Cariboo, and as a consequence, upcountry traders were desperate for goods and willing to pay higher prices. But by September of that same year, the traders, determined not to be caught short again, had built up their stocks, and the rates they were offering were so low that some packers turned their animals out to grass early for the winter.

Although the Cariboo packing season could start any time between March and May, depending on when the snow melted from the trails and the grass had begun to grow along the way, the best months for packing were June, July and August because the trails would generally be dry then. However, any packing done after July had to be routed through areas where ranches and roadhouses could provide hay and grain, because by this time, the roadside grasses on which their pack animals depended for food would generally have withered from lack of rain. The packers would keep their trains operating as long as they could into the fall, but little packing took place during the winter months because blizzards closed most of the trails and snow covered the grass. The toll records for October 1862 show that 103 outfits set out from Lillooet on the trail north, carrying 194,053 pounds (88,020 kilograms) of freight; in November, this had declined to 50 outfits carrying 44,775 pounds (20,339 kilograms); and the number dropped to just 6 outfits carrying 5556 pounds (2520 kilograms) in December.[34]

In late fall, most of the pack trains would head downriver to the "dry belt" south of Soda Creek, where there was less snow on the ground. They settled in for the winter in the small communities of Williams Lake, Chimney Creek, Alkali Lake, Dog Creek, Canoe Creek or Big Bar, with some even travelling as far south as Lillooet.[35] Many of the Mexican packers chose the Nicola Valley to overwinter, and their presence—and eventual retirement there to take up ranching—gave rise to the town of Merritt.

○━┿━○

Mark Sweeten Wade (1858–1929), a doctor and historian, was the author of three books published in his lifetime, but it is his remarkable book *The Cariboo Road*, written in the 1920s but not published until 1979, that describes what Williams Lake was like in the early 1860s:

> In 1861 and 1862 Williams Lake enjoyed a boom. The sittings of the courts of law were held there and it was not until 1863 that it lost that distinction, when court began to be held at Richfield-Barkerville instead.... Williams Lake grew out of the necessities of the times. The old

> pack trails along the Fraser and those to Beaver
> Lake, Quesnel Forks and the creek that made
> the Cariboo famous passed that way, and the
> town sprang into existence before the wag-
> on was mooted. Most of the inhabitants were
> Americans, a large number of whom had come
> from Oregon and California bringing stock of
> all kinds along.[36]

When the Caux brothers first began investing in mules for their pack train, they wintered them in Marble Canyon, which lies midway between Lillooet and Cache Creek. Here the steep limestone walls provided protection from wind and storms, and there was an adequate supply of drinking water in a nearby lake. They also often rested their animals at the mule transfer station established at the Spanish Ranch—so named because its Mexican owner, Juan Tressiera, spoke Spanish. The ranch was about two miles (three kilometres) south of Clinton (also known as Cut-Off Creek) on what is now Lots 267, 268, 269, G.1, Lillooet.[37] This was the meeting point of the trail from Lillooet and the pack trail from Yale via the Fraser Canyon, so Tressiera prospered by growing vegetables to feed travellers and providing barley and hay for their pack animals.

In time, however, the rigors of the long packing trip from Yale to Barkerville convinced the brothers to change their wintering place to Dog Creek, south of Williams Lake, because of the excellent winter forage available there. It was in Dog Creek that they met the Comte de Versepuech, Isadore Gaspard, a Frenchman from the town of Saint-Hippolyte on the French-German border. By 1861, he had established a ranch to grow wheat, and in order to mill it, he went to San Francisco to buy a set of French burr millstones, which he had shipped to Yale. Although there were many established packers in the area, Gaspard enlisted the Caux brothers, fellow Frenchmen, to pack the millstones from Yale to Dog Creek, where his grist mill was soon producing flour for the district. Gaspard imported a larger set of millstones in 1867.[38]

Another Frenchman who came into their lives in these years was Joseph Guichon, who had been born in the village of Chambéry in the Auvergne-Rhône-Alpes region of southeastern France in 1843 and arrived in the Cariboo in March 1864 to make his fortune in the goldfields. He soon discovered—as his three much older brothers had before him—that packing was a far better way to make his fortune, and he hired on with the Caux brothers in 1866. Two years later, although he continued to work for the Caux brothers from time to time, he had earned enough to join his brother Laurent in developing a ranch in the Nicola Valley, gradually expanding it and sometimes competing for pasture land with the adjacent Douglas Lake Cattle Company. Although in time the Guichon brothers became the landed aristocracy of the district, importing the first Hereford cows and building the Quilchena Hotel, Joseph Guichon remained Jean Caux's good friend throughout the years.

THE CARIBOO WAGON ROAD

⌗

By 1862, it had become apparent to the colonial government that trails were not enough to service the burgeoning industries of the Cariboo goldfields. A wagon road was necessary, and Governor Douglas commissioned the Royal Engineers to produce a report on possible routes. That report, delivered a year later by Lieutenant H.S. Palmer, recommended that the road avoid the Harrison-Lillooet route as well as much of the Fraser Canyon by diverting at Lytton into the canyon of the Thompson River. From Ashcroft, it could follow the Bonaparte River to Clinton, and from there, it could be routed along the Fraser, passing close to the Hudson's Bay Company's Fort Alexandria and Quesnellemouth (now Quesnel), before turning towards Cottonwood and continuing on to Richfield and Barkerville. Alternatively, the report advised, the wagon road could follow the existing trail through Beaver Lake and Quesnel Forks, finally reaching Barkerville after crossing the mountains. Palmer, however, recommended the route through Quesnellemouth, even though it was thirty miles (forty kilometres) longer, because it was flatter, easier for animals and packers and had superior feed locations.

The government accepted all of Palmer's recommendations, and in the early spring of 1863, the Royal Engineers set about constructing the two most difficult stretches of the new road—the twelve miles (nineteen kilometres) along the west side of the Fraser River from Yale to Spuzzum and the nine miles (fifteen kilometres) from Cook's Ferry north along the Thompson River—because these sections involved a great deal of rock blasting. A suspension bridge also had to be constructed across the Fraser River at Spuzzum because the road north from there to Lytton had to be built on the east side of the river. The remainder of the project was turned over to private contractors, but owing to the extreme

Jackass Mountain. From 1863 to 1865, construction of the Cariboo Wagon Road ran from Lytton to Barkerville alongside the Thompson, Bonaparte and Fraser Rivers. Although the road design allowed for wagon transport, it was still more economical to deliver supplies by pack train. Image G-00781 courtesy of the Royal BC Museum and Archives

difficulty of the terrain, progress was slow, and that winter, after completing the road as far as Soda Creek, they established a temporary, less strenuous pack trail from there via Quesnellemouth to Richfield. Packers, however, still preferred the old plateau route between these two places because of the abundance of grass and water to be found there, especially in late summer when all the pasturage on the Quesnellemouth-to-Richfield trail had withered.

It was not until the late summer of 1865 that the wagon road was finally completed to Barkerville, but in the meantime the mining picture there had changed—first, because the American Civil War had ended, providing a signal for the last of the American miners to head home, and second, because the small-scale placer mining operations had almost exhausted all the rich surface deposits, and large hydraulic mining companies were beginning to take their place. The new road also allowed more competition into that area from wagon outfits such as Barnard's Express and Stage Lines, although fortunately for the Caux brothers and other packers, the population of the area had also increased dramatically, and only pack trains could deliver the necessary quantities of freight economically.

By 1869, the Caux brothers' pack train had become well-respected on the Yale to Barkerville route because they had learned that the keys to success were speed and reliability: they had to get to their destination as fast as possible without damaging or losing any of their freight but also get in as many runs as possible before winter arrived. That year they made four trips to Barkerville, demonstrated by the road toll collections report for Clinton, which noted that they paid $126 on May 5, $124 on June 26 and $125 on August 17.[39] The September 4, 1869, edition of the *Cariboo Sentinel*, published in Barkerville, noted that the pack trains of Thomas

Due to the rough terrain, a significant amount of rock blasting was required to accommodate wagon passage along the Cariboo Highway. This passage along the Fraser Canyon was photographed in 1898. Image B-04252 courtesy of the Royal BC Museum and Archives

Hutchinson and Henry Bowman, both carrying goods from Yale, had arrived there the previous Wednesday and that the "Caux Bros. train arrived on Thursday [September 2]."[40] On their final trip of the season, they passed through Clinton on October 18 heading north and paid another $120 in tolls.[41] They would not have arrived in Barkerville until mid-November, probably battling early winter conditions to get there.

It was probably the kind of determination displayed by independent packers like the Caux brothers that prompted the Hudson's Bay Company to make its first attempt to sell off its pack trains that year. It also may have seemed that contracting with private outfits for freighting services would be cheaper, but with the completion of the wagon road, there were surplus pack animals in the colony, so they were unable to find buyers. On the plus side, since the colony had acquired a well-engineered north-south connector, more towns, farms and ranches began to develop, providing new customers for the company as well as for pack trains and horse and wagon operations.

Events in the Caux brothers' lives in 1870 and 1871 are well documented in newspapers and government records. According to the Record of Trading Licences at Lytton (1859–71), on May 21, 1870, Jean Caux was issued retail trading licence #5063, allowing him to work as a trader for a period of two months. In a column titled "Road Traffic" in the August 20 issue of Barkerville's *Cariboo Sentinel*, it was noted that the "Caux Bros' train" had arrived from Yale the previous Thursday, August 18."[42] A year later, under "Freight Arriving" in the August 19 issue of the *Sentinel*, readers were advised to expect the imminent arrival of the "Caux Bros pack train with assorted cargoes for different parties."[43] But this August announcement was the last time the Caux pack train was identified in this way. At some point after August 1871, Jean-Pierre Caux vanished from the colony. If his name had not been on the manifest of the *Mercury* in 1857, if he had not taken out mining licence #157 in 1859, and if his signature had not appeared as #28 on a petition in the early 1860s (Jean Caux's signature was #31), his physical presence in British Columbia might be doubted. However, since no death certificate was filed in Victoria, and no newspaper remarked on his passing, it can probably be safely assumed that he returned to France. This, of course, was not a rare occurrence. At least three-quarters of the men who came to British Columbia in the latter part of the nineteenth century did not stay. They had come to make their fortunes and most of them, faced with the realities of life here, left without making it. Fortunately, returning home for Jean-Pierre Caux would not have been as difficult as the brothers' journey to British Columbia had been, because the last spike of the first transcontinental railroad in the United States had been driven in Utah on May 6, 1869.

By the time his brother left, Jean Caux had been in British Columbia for thirteen years, long enough to become known by the nickname "Cataline." It was not unusual for the men and women who had been integrated into the community to be given colourful sobriquets—his Mexican friend Jesus Garcia became known as "Cariboo Pete"—but why Jean Caux was given a nickname and why he became known by this particular one are unanswered questions. There were, however, a number of intriguing theories put forward by those who actually knew him. Judge Henry Castillou said that, since places of origin were often confused in those days, it was possible that he got his nickname because people thought he had come from Catalonia in Spain. He also pointed out that many last names were twisted and misread from the original; his own father, Joseph Castillou, was referred to even in official Canadian census records as Castillion. Trader Martin Starret told interviewer Imbert Orchard that

> his name was Jean Caux, but he used the word
> Cataline. For instance, if a string of hors-
> es [was] going along—or mules—on the trail
> and they'd come to a hill and there'd be about
> ten of them up on this hill and they'd stop and
> get their wind.... Well then, that's holding the
> whole darn train up. Cataline'd be sitting back
> there [on his horse]... and when he'd think it

> was about time for these mules to start again,
> he'd say: "Hey there, Cataline!" Then them old
> mules'd flip their ears back and forward and
> start up then when he'd holler "Cataline!"[44]

Others said the word he yelled at his mules was not "Cataline" but "Catalonia," and that it was just one of the many expletives that he was in the habit of using. His language, most who knew him agreed, was lurid at times, an unforgettable "mixture of polyglot profanity, accompanied by violent gestures,"[45] and he was reputed to be able to swear in seven languages. Judge Castillou insisted that "Cataline spoke very little French, he knew no Spanish, and he had no interpreter unless my dad was with him to explain these things, so he formed a distinctive language between all these Indian languages, the trade language of Chinook, together with the words from the Spanish packers, and English, Scotch, French and Irish. Cataline formed a vocabulary which no one could really understand."[46]

Paddy Carroll, who was just a youth when he met Cataline in 1907, concurred. He told his daughter, Cecille, that

> carrying on a conversation with Cataline was
> next to impossible, for his original Béarnese ac-
> cent was peppered with a smattering of French
> and Spanish. Added to that were his gleanings
> from exchanges with various Indian tribes with
> whom he did business, and he also had adopted
> words from French Canadians, Irish, Germans,
> French, Mexicans, Scots, British and Chinese…
> [and he] swore with great dexterity in all lan-
> guages.

Cataline magnanimously made no distinction among he, she, it, they, his, her, its and theirs—they were all "he." He also acquired two useful words from the Chinese: *maskee*, a common word meaning no matter, without, anyhow, however or in spite of, and *gelow* which means nothing at all but is a marvellously expressive substitute to be used anywhere when one can't quite come up with the right word.[47]

Yet strangely, although most were agreed that Cataline spoke a language that absolutely no one could understand, he was also renowned as a great storyteller, especially around the campfire when the pack train was on the road. And he seems to have been in command of enough English to carry on a very successful packing and trading business, although part of this success was undoubtedly due to his remarkably retentive memory. Judge Castillou recalled that "he knew exactly what was on every one of those 66 horses, he knew exactly the price to charge, he knew exactly where he had to leave his stuff off without any notes whatsoever."

By this time Cataline had also developed some singular personal habits that marked him off from other packers. There was, for example, his strange habit of drinking about three-quarters of a glass of rum, pouring the rest on his hand and rubbing it into his hair. Fur trader George Ogston commented "whether it was the quality of the Hudson's Bay rum he drank, I do not know, but he had a magnificent crop on his head."[48] Nellie English Baker (who was born in 1888 near Cache Creek and died in Quesnel in 1971) recalled going with her father, Doc English, to Cataline's cabin near the Cornwall ranch at Ashcroft. "First time I tasted rum, old Cataline gave me a spoon and I cleaned out his cup. It was sugar

Cataline (right) was known for his peculiar hygiene practices; many who spent time with him noted his habit of rubbing rum in his hair, which some speculated contributed to his signature thick, curly locks. Image B-01202 courtesy of the Royal BC Museum and Archives

and rum, you know."[49] There was also his habit of pulling out a plug of T&B tobacco as he rode along and shaving away at it with his jackknife until he had the fine powder in the palm of his hand, which he snuffed with deep appreciation.

But the thing most people remembered about him was the stiff-bosomed white dress shirt (minus collar and tie) that he always wore with blue denim overalls stuffed into knee-high cowhide boots. Some said he bought a new shirt every time he returned to Ashcroft or Yale and never took it off until he came back for a second load, but others said this was a gross libel—because he was known to buy shirts in Quesnel and later in Hazelton as well. However, his wardrobe never varied, no matter the weather, the season or the temperature. And he never wore socks, although on important occasions he did add a frock coat to his ensemble, which may have been the cause of one titled European inviting him for a drink. But after Cataline had, in his customary manner, drunk three-quarters of his glass of rum, then rubbed the remainder into his hair, the foreigner remarked with some surprise:

> "I have the honor of drinking with the governor, yes?"

> "Catalonia, no! Me, I work!" was Cataline's indignant retort.[50]

(It is certainly possible that this meeting did take place since there was no shortage of titled individuals and younger sons of titled families languishing in British Columbia in those days.)

After thirteen years on the trail, Cataline had become physically tough, and the sun and weather had bronzed him so that on top of his natural swarthy hue, he no longer looked white, and was often mistaken for one of the Mexican packers with whom he frequently consorted. He never slept in a tent, no matter how hard it was raining; he would cut a few branches and lay three blankets over them. Apparently he was also impervious to the cold and slept outdoors even in mid-winter. Sperry Cline had not believed this story to be true until he observed his friend firsthand.

> I had occasion to make a hurried trip to Babine Lake. I had walked all night and just at daybreak I came upon Cataline's camp, which was at the timberline, and it had been a frosty night. He was asleep at the side of the trail, his bed a man-teau (canvas pack cover) spread on the ground. He was fully clothed, even to his spurs, and had no cover, and the small fire which he had started beside him had burned out. I stood for a few minutes watching his deep, steady breathing; his chest rose and fell in regular beat and his hair, beard and clothing were heavily cover[ed] with white frost. He was enjoying a good rest.[51]

According to Cline, Cataline's diet appears to have been as limited as his vocabulary—but just as creative.

> His digestive organs must have been quite equal to his circulation for he lived on a fare that would soon have palled or sickened a normal person. On the trail it was principally bannock and beans, the latter being highly seasoned with pepper. Owing to his limited vocabulary he only spoke of two kinds of meat, bacon and beef. Any game that he might secure along the trail such as deer, rabbits, squirrels or cured meats

were "bacon." In summer he became largely
vegetarian; weeds and herbs of many varieties,
all of which he described as "gooda lettuce,"
were added to his diet and consumed liberally
doused with or soaked in vinegar.[52]

Although his brother's departure had left a hole in Cataline's
life, he was surrounded by friends and business acquaintances.
Many of them had begun life in France and retained an emotional attachment of some sort to their former homeland, and this was
especially evident during the Franco-Prussian War, which began
on July 19, 1870. The French suffered defeat after defeat, including a siege of Paris that ended in several months of famine, before
the war was formally ended with the Treaty of Frankfurt on May
21, 1871. Unfortunately, the conflict didn't end there, because the
citizens of Paris refused to disarm themselves and accept the rule
of the national assembly that had capitulated to the Prussians.
French troops then staged a second siege of Paris in April and
May 1871.

In British Columbia, the general sympathy was with the Pari-
sians, and the *British Colonist* newspaper in Victoria began soliciting
funds for the French Relief Fund; Jean Caux's donation of twenty
dollars appeared in a list printed in the August 31, 1871, issue.[53]
A benefit concert for the relief fund that was held in Barkerville
also accepted "subscriptions" [donations], and his name was listed
there as well, among the donors from Richfield, where he was delivering freight before going on to Barkerville.

THE OMINECA GOLD RUSH OF 1869

❦

The first recorded gold discovery in the Omineca district of northern British Columbia had been made in the summer of 1861 by William Cust and Edward Cary. They had travelled north from Alexandria to the Findlay River area that spring and returned in the fall with sixty ounces of gold. This was just enough encouragement for others to make the same difficult journey over the next five years, but none of them found enough gold to spark a rush. Then in May 1869, a well-financed group of four veteran miners, who became known as the Peace River Prospecting Party, set off from Quesnel for the north by boat via the Fraser, Nechako and Stuart Rivers. They then continued on foot beside Stuart, Trembleur and Takla Lakes. Their stated aim was to explore and prospect. That fall, however, after finding gold on Vital Creek, which flows into the Omineca River, they returned to Quesnel, where they reported they'd had little success. But when they announced they were returning to Vital Creek to spend the winter, suspicions were aroused and gold rush fever swept through the mining community once again.

Extremely heavy snows in the winter of 1869–70 meant surface mining was impossible. The shafts dug by the newcomers produced little gold and had to be abandoned, but few of the men were discouraged. Spring brought more miners north, following the route used by the Peace River Prospecting Party, and by June another four hundred men had arrived. James Germansen struck out on his own and found gold on another small tributary of the Omineca—the stream was subsequently named after him—and soon everyone had flocked from Vital Creek to this new area, and many excellent claims were being worked up and down both sides of the creek. Two sawmills were constructed to provide lumber to build sluice boxes and homes for the miners, and before winter arrived again, a settlement called Omineca City had blossomed.

Another group of men made their way north in the spring of 1871, raising the population of the area to around 1200, and in July, gold was found on nearby Manson's Creek, then on Blackjack, Kildare, Mosquito, Slate and Lost Creeks as well as in Nugget Gulch. But by this time, there was a serious provisioning problem since there was only one trader in the whole area, a man named Elmore who had set up shop in Omineca City. He had little stock and no tools for sale, and his food prices were sky-high because, with such a short working season, packers had been reluctant to come this far north over such primitive trails. There was also the problem of finding a market after they got there unless the goods had been specifically ordered. They had all heard the story of the packer who had brought in a loaded train "on spec" via Fort St. James in the summer of 1870, planning to sell his goods at the mining camps along Vital Creek, but at Takla Landing he had learned that "the diggings [on Vital Creek] were exhausted and all the miners had departed for Germansen Creek. He was forced to dump his goods outside Takla Landing."[54]

The supply situation improved somewhat in the late spring of 1871, when Captain William Meade brought in a pack train from Hazelton via Takla Landing, and that summer a road was constructed from the landing to Fall River and a nine-mile-long (fourteen-kilometre-long) portage cleared from the Fraser River to Summit Lake, encouraging more packers to come north. It was now obvious that Hazelton was best placed to be the base of pack train activity to the Omineca goldfields because the right-of-way for the Collins Overland Telegraph line, although abandoned in 1866, provided convenient access to it from Quesnel. Soon a pack trail had been established from Hazelton towards Babine and Takla Lakes and into the Omineca River region, but it was narrow and frequently blocked by fallen trees. But on July 20, 1871, British Columbia signed on as a province of Canada, and the new provincial government contracted Robert Cunningham and Thomas Hankin, who ran a small trading post in Hazelton, to improve the trail between Gitanmaax and Babine Lake. The work was completed just in time for the Skeena gold rush of 1871 and 1872.[55]

Cataline was one of the many packers who made the trip to the Omineca goldfields in the late summer of 1871. He had delivered freight to Richfield before going on to Barkerville, arriving there on August 19. While in Barkerville, he had been approached by the owner of a local brewery to bring a load of freight from Yale for him. The brewer, however, refused to give him a written contract, and Cataline decided instead to accept a contract to take provisions to Messrs. Smith and Sterling who had opened a trading post and saloon on Germansen Creek. By now his train of mules had grown to sixty animals, and in late August, he went to Quesnel, which had taken over from Alexandria as the Hudson's Bay Company's main Cariboo distribution centre for goods going north. There he loaded up with trade goods plus the freight for Smith and Sterling. Instead of using Captain Meade's new and still difficult route via Hazelton, he followed the trail north from Quesnel through Fort St. James, which had been established by the miners. As described by Lizette Hall in her book *The Carrier, My People*, after leaving Quesnel the trail went by way of

> Goose Lake and Stoney Creek where the pack trains turned north to the Nechako River. They crossed at Noonla, two miles west of Vanderhoof. In low water the mules forded the river. A family from Tatchek lived at Noonla, and during high water this family took the freight across the river in a dugout canoe, and the mules swam across. From Noonla the trail went 18 miles [29 kilometres] to a place called "Old Ferry" on the Stuart River, 25 miles [40 kilometres] from Fort St. James. Ezra Evans owned and operated the ferry scow there. He whip-sawed the lumber for the scow himself by tying a rock to the lower end of the saw and sawing various lengths of two- by twelve-foot [sixty-one centimetres by three-and-a-half metres] planks. The scow was 30 feet [9 metres] wide and 50 feet [15 metres] long…. He strung a stout rope across the river and also put a pier at the river centre, and he took the ferry across hand over hand to the opposite side. He took 20 mules with packs each trip.
>
> [The packers then] followed the shore of [Stuart] Lake to the source of the Stuart River.

> Here the packhorses forded the river just above
> Long Island in low water, but in high water they
> had to swim while the freight was taken across
> in dugout canoes or by barges. Then the pack
> trains went on the south side of Mount Pope,
> up on the north side of Tatchie River, Trem-
> bleur Lake, Middle River, Tatlah [Takla] Lake
> and then northeast to Manson and Tom Creek
> and the gold diggings.[56]

It was the beginning of October before Cataline and his pack train arrived at Germansen Creek. The receipt he signed on October 5, 1871, testifies to the fact that he received $2900.92 from Smith and Sterling in return for delivering "8 kegs of S.C. sugar, 500 [bags of] rice, 2 boxes of P. [pearl] barley, a box of split peas and 3 c [probably cartons] of peaches." The receipt also notes that the delivery was "short" for some barley and sugar and a bottle of brandy.[57]

For most of the miners and packers—including Cataline— winter in the Omineca was a totally new experience, and they were unprepared for its severity. That year, when it came on earlier and even more severely than usual, the packers barely made it out alive. Their animals, in many cases, did not make it out at all. They either froze or starved or died in accidents. The December 9 issue of the *Mainland Guardian*, published in New Westminster, reported on the final outcome of that cruel journey:

> We are indebted to Mr. Gillis [of the Vital
> Creek saloon owners Brown and Gillis] for the
> following information. There were about 40
> men together who arrived from Omineca at

Fort George [in November]. The ice having become so thick as to render boating further impossible, they hauled up their boats 8 miles below and attempted to accomplish the rest of the way to Quesnelmouth on foot. [River boat pilot Edmund C.] Shepherd found a canoe in the canyon and picked up [Peter C.] Dunlevy, [Joseph] Guichon, [Thaddeus] Harper and [Abraham] Barlow with whom he came down and arrived on 21st ult. [November 21]. [Rufus] Sylvester arrived on the 22nd with 7 or 8 others, and on the 23rd Cicery, J. Curry and 5 or 6 others in a canoe, which they found in the river on the way down. They left 18 men short of provisions with a very poor prospect of getting out of the snow, amongst them William Pinchbeck, Al Thorpe and J. Sellers. The people of Quesnelmouth immediately fitted out a boat with 500 lbs [227 kg] of provisions, manned by [Barkerville miners] Jim Loring, Jackson, Butler and W. Downey, which was dispatched to the assistance of the stragglers.

[Packer] J.B. Brian arrived at Quesnelmouth by trail. He had lost all his animals (21 horses) but 5 when he left them; he determined to return with provisions for his men. Terry lost all his animals. Hutchison lost 18 out of 81. Catalan [Cataline] lost 30 of his mules, and Mitchell 6. Dancing Bill [Latham] lost all his, and Billy Walsh is supposed to have fared no better.

Hazelton was well positioned during the Omenica gold rush due to its convenient access from Quesnel. Many packers were unprepared for the severe winters in Omenica, and many pack animals, including thirty of Cataline's mules (shown here outside Hazelton's HBC outpost) were lost to the cold. Image A-03048 courtesy of the Royal BC Museum and Archives

> Sleighing was good as far as the Bonaparte
> [River], and wheels were used afterwards. The
> snow was deep enough from Boothroyds down
> for sleighs. Yeates, the telegraph operator at
> Soda Creek, had a severe task to keep the line
> in order but was exerting himself to the utmost
> to preserve the connection.[58]

General Sir William Francis Butler, who had been sent on re-connaissance for the army in that area in 1873, added a postscript to the story:

> Suddenly, on their return march, the winter
> broke; horses and mules perished miserably
> along the forest trail. At length the Fraser River
> was reached, a few canoes were obtained, but
> the ice was fast filling in the river. The men
> crowded into the canoes till they were filled to
> the edge; three wretched miners could find no
> room; they were left on the shore to their fate;
> their comrades pushed away. Two or three days
> later the three castaways were found frozen stiff
> on the inhospitable shore.[59]

The Omineca gold rush was short-lived, peaking in 1871, and within a year, Germansen and Manson Creeks were the only ones being worked. General Butler, who saw Germansen Creek in 1873, wrote:

> Late on the evening of the 20th of May I
> reached the mining camp of Germansen, three
> miles south of the Omineca River. A queer place

was this mining camp of Germansen, the most northern and remote of all the mines on the American continent. Deep in the bottom of a valley, from whose steep sides the forest had been cleared or burned off, stood some dozen or twenty well-built wooden houses; a few figures moved in the dreary valley, ditches and drains ran along the hillsides, and here and there men were at work with pick and shovel in the varied toil of gold-mining.[60]

By 1874, only around sixty miners were left in the Omineca.

Cataline and the Law

Cataline's loss of half his animals was a devastating financial and emotional blow. He headed for Barkerville with his crew and the remains of his mule team, and there, in late November 1871, he was sued for $500 in damages by Nicholas Cunio (also known as Nicola Cuneo). Cunio accused him of breach of contract for failing to deliver a load of freight from Yale to his saloon and brewery in Barkerville. George Wallace, who had established Barkerville's *Cariboo Sentinel* in order "to disseminate mining intelligence and eradicate official abuses of power,"[61] covered the County Court hearing held on Thursday, November 30, in Barkerville. In the December 2 edition of the paper, he told his readers that this case "was a very important one as affecting the validity of verbal contracts."[62]

Cunio was represented by the formidable McGill University trained lawyer George Anthony Walkem, who had just been elected to BC's first legislative assembly as the member for Cariboo and was destined to serve as BC's premier from 1874 to 1876 and 1878 to 1882. Cataline was defended by a pair of up-country lawyers, Davie and Park (the latter was reputed to have a drinking problem), and they arranged for a French translator to help him during the trial. Although at this point he certainly knew enough English to conduct

Mr. and Mrs. Nicholas Cunio were embroiled in a legal battle with Cataline over his failure to deliver goods to their saloon and brewery in Barkerville. Image H-06518 courtesy of the Royal BC Museum and Archives

a successful business, he had a strong accent and probably felt more comfortable dealing with such serious legal business in French.

On the stand, the brewery owner told a convoluted tale that began with a meeting with Cataline in mid-August. At this time, Cunio had told Cataline that he had contracted with a packer named M.C. Davis to bring 15,000 or 16,000 pounds (6804 or 7257 kilograms) of freight from the warehouse of Kimball & Gladwin in Yale to Barkerville for him. When Cataline told him he had heard that Davis had sold his pack train, Cunio offered the job to Cataline. After settling on a price of 12½¢ a pound, Cataline agreed to pack his freight from Yale, but over the next two days, he asked several times whether they should have a written contract. Cunio said they had both agreed it was not necessary since they had known one another a long time. Subsequently he telegraphed Kimball & Gladwin to deliver the goods to Cataline when he came to Yale, but a few days later, they telegraphed back to say that Cataline had advised them not to keep the freight for him because he was going to Germanson Creek. As a result, Cunio was obliged to find other means of transporting his goods and lost both money and time. He was followed on the stand by five witnesses who all swore they had heard Cataline promise to bring Cunio's freight from Yale to Barkerville.

After hearing the witnesses, Cataline's lawyer, Mr. Davie, moved for a non-suit on the grounds that Cataline was not a "common carrier" who was bound to carry goods for all parties. He said a contract must be obligatory on both parties, but in this case, there was nothing to bind either party because nothing had been done under agreement. His colleague, Mr. Park, added that it was a maxim of the law that no action could lie on a naked contract, and this contract was definitely naked, because the plaintiff had not shown payment of monies, delivery of goods or a written agreement. Walkem called the defence's arguments absurd and contrary to common sense and justice. The judge agreed; there was, he said, good cause for court action to continue.

Mr. Davie then opened the case for the defence, and Cataline, taking the stand, told the court through his interpreter that

> Cunio asked me if I had seen Davis at Quesn- elmouth, and if I knew what he was doing and where he was going. I told him I did not know but had heard that he had sold his train; the plaintiff asked where I was going and said that, if I would go to Yale, he would give me the freight if Davis did not take it, and he would telegraph to Kimball & Gladwin to that effect. I said I would go if he would bind himself by a written contract, but he would not give one; he said if I went to Yale, I could bring a load from there at 12½¢, and if I made up my mind to go I should telegraph down, but I said I might go to Stuart's Lake; I would have preferred a load from Yale if secured, but I telegraphed on Au- gust 20 to Kimball & Gladwin not to keep the freight as I was going to Germansen Creek....[63]

Park then argued that the plaintiff's suffering was due to his own negligence since, even if Davis had sold his train of mules, he might have "brought the goods by another conveyance." The reason, Park said, that Cunio had not been willing to give Cataline a contract was that he would have then had to pay Davis $500 as a penalty for breaking his contract with him. It now became evident that Walkem viewed this case as a means to bring all packers into line because he countered Park's statement by saying that "packers should be compelled to fulfil their contracts, the breach of which had been a fruitful source of litigation for the last ten years. Where, as here, there were mutual promises and mutual considerations, there was no necessity for writings."[64]

However, after deliberating for just half an hour, the jury, which was composed of five local men—James A. Laidlaw (foreman), Henry Cline, F. Perret, J.C. McMillan and Benjamin Springer—returned a verdict in favour of the defendant. For Cataline, this should have been reason for celebration, but unfortunately the repercussions from his decision not to carry Cunio's goods were not over. In the Richfield police court on Saturday, December 2, he was charged with perjury "on the information of N. Cunio," a perjury that was allegedly committed during the County Court trial "by swearing falsely that he had not made an express agreement with the complainant to bring a quantity of freight from Yale."[65] The Richfield magistrate decided there was sufficient evidence to warrant the case being sent before the grand jury at the next assizes, and Cataline was forced to provide bail in the form of two sureties for $1000. Since he had lost thirty of his sixty mules just weeks earlier, this was a crippling blow.

The final chapter of this story occurred on Wednesday, June 5, 1872, when Cataline appeared before his old friend Judge Matthew Baillie Begbie at the Richfield assizes on the perjury charge. There was some wrangling between the lawyers, but in the end, the grand jury returned a decision of "No bill" in the case of Regina v. Caux, and Cataline's ordeal was at last over. By this time, Cunio no longer owned the brewery and saloon, having sold them to a man called Vaillancour, so it is quite possible that Cunio's determination to get his "pound of flesh" from Cataline had been entirely due to the rough state of his own finances.

There was, however, a postscript of sorts to this story. It was told in 1959 by Cataline's friend, the former police officer Sperry Cline, who was the son of one of the jurors at Cataline's first trial. He wrote that

> Cataline had moved to the Cariboo and had squatted on a piece of pasture land where he kept his stock. As civilization advanced, Cariboo ranches became valuable and someone protested his right to the land on the grounds that he was not a citizen. Begbie had received news of the pending court action [against Cataline] and was on his way to Richfield to hold court. On his way up the Cariboo Road he met Cataline, convened an impromptu court and naturalized him or, as Cataline described it, he "come Canada boy." When the petition was read in court in Richfield, Begbie said in a rather surprised voice, "What's this? Cataline is a citizen naturalized by my court. Proceed with the next case."[66]

It would seem that Begbie had remembered that long-ago day when Cataline had been there to "standa by the judge."

The Stikine and Cassiar Gold Rushes

꒐━꒐

As the Omineca diggings were playing out in the early 1870s, miners began moving into the rugged country even farther north and west, first to the Stikine River and then into the Cassiar district. Due to the harsh climate and difficult winters, the population in that region in the 1870s was no more than a thousand people, almost all of them Indigenous, with the exception of a few fur traders. But it was not completely new territory for prospectors: gold had been found in 1861 on the Anuk River near its confluence with the Stikine by Alexander "Buck" Choquette. His find had resulted in a brief rush of prospectors entering the district via Fort Stikine (now Wrangell, Alaska), a trading post established by the Hudson's Bay Company on an island at the mouth of the river. When the subsequent returns from the creeks flowing into the Stikine proved disappointing, prospectors withdrew from the area for the next decade.

A few years later, however, something occurred that would draw miners back. The American entrepreneur Perry Collins persuaded the Western Union Telegraph Company to finance the construction of a telegraph line from San Francisco north through British Columbia and Alaska, then across the Bering Strait to Russia and finally to Europe. By July 1866, Collins's telegraph cable had been strung from San Francisco to New Westminster, from there to Quesnel, and then on to Kispiox, about ten miles (sixteen kilometres) north of Hazelton, when the whole project came to a complete halt. Collins's line had been made redundant by the successful laying of a cable across the Atlantic Ocean. In the aftermath, Western Union had been happy to lease all of its now useless British Columbia assets to the colonial government, and when BC became a province of Canada in July 1871, the Dominion government assumed responsibility for the line. A decade later, the government would buy up the assets, and the Canadian Pacific Railway would sign a maintenance contract for the section of line lying between Ashcroft and Quesnel. Part of that maintenance was to rebuild some of the most hastily constructed sections.[67] The line north of Quesnel was never a government priority.

Far more important to the mining and packing industries, however, was the fact that before laying down their tools, Collins's crews had surveyed and cleared a primitive route for the line from Kispiox all the way north to the new settlement of Telegraph Creek at the head of navigation on the Stikine River. It was this trail through the wilderness that encouraged prospectors to look at the area again, and in the summer of 1872, Henry Thibert and Angus McCulloch found gold on a stream (subsequently called Thibert Creek) that drains from the west into the northern end of Dease Lake. It was a rich find, with the two prospectors taking out as much as three ounces per pan, but the next year an even richer find was made to the north on McDame Creek, where the largest nugget ever discovered in British Columbia was found.

Construction of the Western Union Telegraph Company's telegraph line from San Francisco to Hazelton resulted in newly cleared routes that encouraged prospectors to return to Telegraph Creek, resulting in renewed exploration and the discovery of gold, including the largest nugget ever found in BC, in the surrounding creeks. Image A-01572 courtesy of the Royal BC Museum and Archives

As the news got out, hordes of miners once again headed north, some of them up the telegraph right-of-way. But Captain William Moore and his three sons, who operated a steamboat on the Stikine River, convinced the British Columbia government that a pack trail was needed from Telegraph Creek northeast to Dease Lake, where the mining settlements of Laketon, Porter Landing and Centreville had already sprung up; he was given the charter to build it in exchange for the right to collect a freight toll. His trail began twelve miles (twenty kilometres) downriver from Telegraph Creek at Glenora Landing, where freight and passengers were off-loaded, and by the time the first big wave of Cassiar gold rush miners arrived in the spring of 1874, Moore had completed it as far as Dease Lake. The government took control of it a year later after miners complained of its unsatisfactory condition.

Despite Cataline's recent loss of pack animals in Omineca and his Barkerville courtroom battles, he was back to packing by the end of 1872, but now he was partnered with another Frenchman, Sauveur Buc (whom the *Colonist* newspaper persisted in spelling "Buck.") Buc, who was about a dozen years older than Cataline, had been born in Mont Louis in the south of France, close to Cataline's birthplace in Béarn. By the summer of 1873 (or at the latest the spring of 1874), the two men were taking their mule trains north into the Cassiar goldfields with provisions for the miners there. In 1875, the Victoria *Colonist* reported that there were at least eight or nine pack trains travelling the Telegraph Creek to Dease Lake trail to service the Cassiar mining camps. They included John Callbreath, who had three pack trains, plus the Caux-Buc partnership, and "Turke, Buckley, Hart and Spanish Frank Dominez." While most of these packers would have shipped their animals by steamboat to Wrangell and then transferred them to smaller boats for the journey up the Stikine, Cataline and Buc had been working out of Hazelton prior to coming to Cassiar and had only to take their animals farther north over the telegraph right-of-way. Unfortunately for them, the provincial government had encouraged those driving beef cattle north to the mining camps to use this route as well, so much of it had been reduced to a quagmire.

Pack animals were shipped by steamboat to Fort Stikine (now Wrangell, Alaska), located on an island at the mouth of the Stikine River, and then transferred to small boats for the journey inland. Image B-07439 courtesy of the Royal BC Museum and Archives

Although most of these packers were old hands at the business and had also operated in Omineca, once again they seem to have been unprepared for the possibility of bitterly cold winters, and during the exceptionally severe winter of 1875–76, they lost most or all of their animals. These losses were mainly from starvation since the snow was too deep to bring in extra hay and grain to feed the animals, although a *Colonist* report in March 1876 said that animals wintered in Wrangell were "doing well." The same issue of that paper advised that "Mr. Cataline" had recently arrived in Victoria on the little mail steamer *California*, which had just put into port from Sitka and Wrangell.[68] With the beginning of the packing season still at least a month off, he was probably seeking a brief respite from the harsh Cassiar weather while Buc took care of their pack animals.

The height of the Cassiar gold rush came during the summer of 1876. By this time, nearly 2000 men were at work in the diggings north of Dease Lake. Although the amount of gold they took out did not compare to that yielded by either the Fraser River or Cariboo gold rushes, it is estimated that the Dease River alone yielded about $1.5 million. The *Colonist* of November 2, 1876, summarizing the packers' situation as they entered that winter, reported that

> Cataline, who has a place near 4-mile (or Miller's Flats), and Buck are… well supplied [with feed for their animals]. Turke's barley is at the H.B.Co.'s post, 90 miles [144 kilometres] below Glenora, and it will be difficult to get the mules through [to the post] before the river freezes. [In fact, Turke lost most of his pack animals, as he was unable to get them to the HBC post.] Buckley has cut hay about 60 miles [97 kilometres] from Glenora and will attempt to winter his mules without grain.[69]

Cataline and Buc were still in the Cassiar area in 1877–78 since they are listed in the "Northwest Coast/Cassiar" section of *The Guide to the Province of British Columbia* for that period as "Catline & Buc" of Dease Creek. In fact, they remained in the Cassiar area for another three winters packing provisions from Glenora to the mining camps.

FAMILY TIES

In September 1878, Cataline was in Telegraph Creek when Father Edwin M.I. Harris, a member of the Oblates of Mary Immaculate, visited the town to administer the sacraments to Catholics living there. Father Harris performed two baptisms on that occasion, although he didn't register them until November, when he returned to his base at St. Peter's Church in New Westminster. The second of these baptisms, #113 in the St. Peter's register, took place on September 23 for "Mary Clemence, aged 8 months, daughter of John Caux (Frenchman) and Lucy, an Indian woman of Sticks [Tahltan] tribe." The register gives no last name for Lucy, but in those days it was not uncommon for First Nations people to be given no surnames in official documents. The name of the child's sponsor is difficult to decipher but could be P. McEntee.[70]

Since Mary Clemence (later known by her second name, Clemence) was eight months old at her baptism, she would have been born in January 1878 and therefore conceived in the spring of 1877, just before Cataline began packing for another season in the Cassiar. He was by then about forty years old. While he acknowledged Lucy's child as his own, there is no record of a marriage between himself and Lucy, probably because he was already involved in another relationship.

The other woman in his life was Amelia Paul, the daughter of Chief Kowpelst (Telxkn) of the Nlaka'pamux people of Spuzzum and sister to Chief James Paul (Xixne). Amelia was born in about 1852, so she was about fifteen years younger than Cataline, and at the time of Mary Clemence's birth she and Cataline already had two children together—Rhoda (Cecw'etkʷuⱼ, born around 1877 in Spuzzum, and William Benjamin (Kʷespaxan), born around 1878 "in a log house on the Cariboo Road a few hundred yards upriver from Shwimp,"[71] which was near the north bank of Spuzzum Creek. When Amelia later married Paul Joseph York, William Benjamin, her son with Cataline, took his stepfather's surname.

Although Cataline drifted out of Amelia's life, he tried to maintain contact with their children, but the transient life of a packer made this contact only intermittent and frequently very unsatisfactory. Annie York recalled her father, William Benjamin, speaking about the sound of the pack train bells that announced Cataline's approach:

> My father would be watching by the fence, and Cataline would say to the pack train to keep going, and he would come down and give money to my father, but my father wouldn't take it because he didn't know [this man was] his father. And every time [Cataline] came he would buy clothes for his children. They say that he was a most generous man. But my father couldn't use that name, Caux, because my grandmother was not married to him…. [Cataline] came in 1891 and gave Auntie [Rhoda] a shawl and money and a gold chain. My father was up in

> the hills when he came, and [Cataline] wanted
> to see my father, but he wasn't there.[72]

Since there was no school in Spuzzum, Rhoda and a younger sister named Clara were enrolled in All Hallows Residential
School in Yale, which was established in late 1884 by the Anglican
Sisters of All Hallows of Ditchingham, Norfolk, England, as a
school for "Indians and half-breed girls." It was supported by the
church's Society for the Propagation of Christian Knowledge as
well as by the Dominion government. Most of the girls were Nlaka'pamux, but there were also girls from the Líl'wat, Secwepémc
and Tsilhqot'in communities. The curriculum the first year after
the school was founded consisted of reading, arithmetic, needle-
work, scripture and domestic work, although it was expanded a
year later to include history, grammar and geography. A few years
later, All Hallows added an exclusive boarding school for girls
of European descent who paid an annual tuition fee. The two
schools shared the same property and the same teachers, but the
students were kept separate, except when attending chapel. The
difference in instruction seems not to have been so much in the
subjects covered as in the time allowed for them and in the emphasis on housekeeping skills for the Indigenous students. Cataline's
daughter Rhoda probably began attending All Hallows shortly after the school opened in 1884; her sister Clara would later recall
first attending when she was eight, which would have been about
1889. Clara spoke no English when she began school, although all
classes were conducted in English.

Cataline had also arranged for his daughter Clemence to be
enrolled in school, but she was far younger when she started than
either Rhoda or Clara. In January 1881, when she was just three
years old, she was taken south from Telegraph Creek to Victoria to

become a student/boarder at the Roman Catholic academy founded by the Sisters of Saint Ann of Lachine, Quebec. While it seems an unconscionably young age to place a child in a boarding school, her enrolment can probably be explained by the fact that Cataline and his partner, Sauveur Buc, were preparing to leave the north. The Cassiar gold rush was essentially over, and there was no longer enough work in that region to keep their pack trains busy.

Cataline's choice of this school would have been largely influenced by his friend Nellie Cashman. She had turned up in Laketon in the Cassiar in 1874 to set up a boarding house for miners, but when she arrived, she had already had a long and colourful career as a miner, prospector and grubstaker as well as a boarding-house keeper and restaurateur. In the Cassiar, she was most remembered for her constant fundraising for the Sisters of St. Ann's hospital-building project in Victoria; she had delivered $500 to the sisters after her first winter in the Cassiar.

The first four sisters had arrived in Victoria in 1858, and they opened their academy in 1871 as a "finishing" school for the "white" girl children of the colony. As a result, the curriculum concentrated on the moral and domestic training deemed suitable for young ladies. A "select division" of students were also taught French and fine arts. Towards the turn of the twentieth century, practical subjects were introduced for a separate "general curriculum," which gradually developed into a commercial school for the training of secretaries.

The census for the James Bay Ward of the City of Victoria in 1881 lists all the girls attending St. Ann's, and "Clemence Coxe," born in British Columbia about 1878, Roman Catholic, was the youngest of them; the oldest was seventeen. A few of the girls in the school were listed as American and two were listed as "half breed," but most were of European heritage. Clemence was enrolled as French, and by that stroke of the pen, she lost her Indigenous heritage entirely.

Clemence's mother must have been persuaded that attending St. Ann's was the best thing for her child, as she appears to have accompanied Clemence to Victoria. The 1881 census for the Johnson Street Ward in Victoria lists an "Indian woman" named Lucy. She was forty years old and had been born in Tongass, BC, a village that lay at the mouth of the Stikine (it now lies within Alaska's Tongass National Park). Although Clemence was baptised as a Roman Catholic, this Lucy is listed as a Wesleyan Methodist; however, the decision to have her baptised by Father Harris would have been Cataline's since he was a Catholic. During the four years that Clemence remained at St. Ann's Academy, Cataline paid a monthly fee of fifteen dollars. In 1886, she transferred to St. Ann's Convent in Duncan, which later became known as Providence Farm.[73] The records show that on November 26, 1887, she took her first communion.[74]

The end of the Caux-Buc partnership was formalized in a legal advertisement in the *British Colonist* newspaper on April 12, 1882. Under the heading "Copartnership Dissolved," it advised that

> the partnership heretofore existing between Sauveur Buc and Jean Caux, trading in Cassiar under the name of Caux & Buc, has this day been dissolved by mutual consent. Saveur Buc is hereby authorized to collect all debts due the late firm and will also pay all liabilities.

It was signed by Jean Caux and Sauveur Buc and witnessed by lawyer M. Camsusa.[75]

The relationship between the two men, however, seems to have continued in a congenial way because Buc, who retired to Lytton after the partnership ended, often paid Clemence's school fees at St. Ann's on Cataline's behalf. He died on March 10, 1886; he was sixty-one years old.

THE CANADIAN PACIFIC RAILWAY

◦━━◆━━◦

Although Prime Minister John A. Macdonald had promised the people of British Columbia a transcontinental railway within ten years of the province's entry into Confederation in 1871, it was not until February 1881 that Parliament finally passed the Railway Bill that would enable its construction. Then, in order to expedite the work—and avoid the possibility of British Columbia seceding from Confederation—construction of the line was contracted out section by section across the country. The most difficult and dangerous part of the entire line—the section running from Emory Bar, four miles (6.4 kilometres) west of Yale, up the Fraser and Thompson canyons to Savona's Ferry on Kamloops Lake—was taken on by a thirty-seven-year-old American engineer, Andrew Onderdonk. His task included blasting four major tunnels and a score of smaller ones through the solid granite mountains north of Yale, building dozens of trestles, bridges and retaining walls through the canyons, preparing the right-of-way and laying the track.

After Onderdonk set up his headquarters in Yale and began survey work in May 1880, he was faced with a dearth of pick-and-shovel labourers to construct the right-of-way. He resolved this problem the same way the American railway builders had dealt with it—by importing as many as 6500 labourers from southeastern China, where overpopulation and a shortage of land were strong incentives for young men to accept work abroad. The Chinese labourers were also cheap to employ because they accepted two-thirds to one-half what Europeans were paid. These workers, plus another 4000 of European stock, were housed in work camps along the right-of-way.

The next problem for Onderdonk was the transportation of supplies and equipment to the construction sites. Everything from steel tracks to food for the work crews had to be brought upriver by steamer from New Westminster, unloaded at Emory Bar, then packed from there farther and farther each day as the line progressed. As a result, he began offering contracts to pack train owners, and it was the promise of this steady work that had lured Cataline south from the Cassiar in the spring of 1881. By the following spring, his name was appearing regularly on the lists of road tolls reported in the *Inland Sentinel*. In the May 4, 1882, issue, J. Canx (Caux) was reported to have paid a toll on April 25 for hauling 7200 pounds (3266 kilograms) for Onderdonk up the Cariboo Wagon Road.[76] His name appears again in the May 11 issue of the paper for paying tolls for hauling 5286 pounds (2398 kilograms) on May 1 and another 1940 pounds (880 kilograms) on May 3, both for the railway.[77]

But packing had changed from the early days of the Fraser River gold rush when mules had been the preferred pack animal because, as well as being able to pack more weight than horses, they were more agile and less apt to stumble on the rough trails. Now, as roads replaced trails, agility was less of a factor, and as mules became more and more expensive and difficult to obtain, instead of being used as pack animals, they were employed most often to pull wagons. A newspaper report from the early 1880s illustrates this change:

> A short time since we advertised in our columns the 12-mule team of Messrs. Burns & McKane for sale. The outfit was sold... to Mr. U. Nelson of this place for £2,200. The mules and wagons were brought to Yale last week, and Mr. Nelson divided the big team into two six-mule teams, with a large and small wagon each.[78]

By the early 1880s, when the CPR began construction in British Columbia, there were hundreds of freight wagons on the roads, some drawn by mules, but most drawn by horses. Those of the British Columbia Express Company carried both passengers and freight, but most were simply open wagons, and their drivers picked up contracts wherever possible. There were still mule pack trains on the trails—the Hudson's Bay Company owned a thirty-animal pack train based in Hazelton—but the average pack train had come to consist of more horses than mules, including Cataline's.

Tom Carolan, who was interviewed by Imbert Orchard in the 1960s, recalled a story that demonstrated Cataline's innate knowledge of his horses.

> I've heard a story of him one time crossing the river at Stony Creek [nine kilometres southeast of Vanderhoof]. He was crossing a small river there and he was loaded with sugar—he had several animals loaded with brown sugar. It was a very hot day and, of course, these were horses. He had warned the Chinese never to

load the horses with sugar because a horse on
a hot day would lay down in the water where a
mule wouldn't. There were several horses that
the packer had loaded with this sugar and they
were crossing this shallow, muddy river. It was a
very hot day and a couple of the horses decided
when they got out in the middle of the river
they were going to lay down. They say the language that came out of Cataline was part of his
swearing in seven languages when these horses
started up the trail and the sugar... syrup was
running out of the pack bags! He was very un-
happy about it.[79]

For Cataline, finding good horses for his pack trains was not
a problem. He had as good an eye for horses as he had for mules.
George Ogston, who knew him between 1903 and 1910, said of
him that "he was a wizard with horses and mules and understood
their whims and vagaries as no other man could."[80] And William
Manson credited him with knowing "the game of horse-packing
thoroughly.... He got the very last ounce of work out of his animals, but he would have every consideration for them if they were
sick.... If a mule had a little bit of a sore back, he would put sand
on it; he told me it kept the flies off."[81] And he had always impressed with his own choice of saddle horses—"handsome, well-
bred animals, their saddles and bridles of the finest leather lavishly
trimmed with silver."[82]

Cataline's principal difficulty while working for Onderdonk was finding good men to ride herd on his pack animals
because it was such a physically demanding job. A man had to
have strength and endurance just to be constantly lifting the

Cataline was known for his preference of hiring men of Indigenous and Chinese descent for his crew, many of whom went on to purchase animals and start their own pack trains under his leadership. Image I-51525 courtesy of the Royal BC Museum and Archives

packs onto the animals' backs. And there was no "normal" piece of cargo; parcels could weigh several hundred pounds and they were all shapes and sizes, some of them extremely awkward to load. By the time he began packing for the CPR in 1881, he seldom hired white men anymore because of their fondness for alcohol. By then, many of his crew were Indigenous men because he found them to be good, steady workers. Some Indigenous men who learned packing techniques by working for him later purchased mules and horses and started their own pack trains.

But Cataline also preferred Chinese workers, some of whom had come to British Columbia as miners, others as railway workers; he found them to be most reliable and hard-working, and he could count on them to stay on the job until it was finished. In fact, for many years his chief lieutenant or *segundo* was a Chinese man known only by the name of "Pretty" who would handle one pack train while Cataline himself took the other.[83] And according to Charles Gordon, an old-timer in Ashcroft, another Chinese man named Bin Lo kept Cataline's accounts—in Chinese.[84] Both men had arrived as miners during the Fraser River gold rush and stayed on.

C.B. "Bill" Bailey told the story of how, as a boy, he had come upon Cataline and his crew camped on one side of the Cariboo Road and, noticing how many Chinese packers were working for him, asked why this was so.

> He looked down at me for a second, grunted once, and went on with his work. I stood first on one foot and then the other, watching him, curious to learn whether that grunt signified that there would be no answer to my question. When he had finished his task, he turned and asked, "You Billy Bailey's boy?"
>
> I nodded assent. I also gathered that if I hadn't been W's son, I'd have probably been told that it was not my business—which it wasn't, of course. However, Cataline assured me that the Chinese were d—d good packers. He also insisted that the whites and Indians were good packers too. Then he went on to explain why he preferred the Chinese.

> ...when a stampede was on, they [Indig-
> enous workers] all wanted to quit and attend
> it. As for the whites, when they arrived in town
> after a long trip, many of them got drunk. Of-
> ten he had to wait two or three days while they
> sobered up before he could hit the trail again.
> But he could always rely on John Chinaman to
> be on the job.[85]

When construction of the CPR was complete, many Chinese men were left jobless. And to make it worse, after 1884 they were no longer able to obtain Crown land, which explains why so many became shopkeepers. Beginning in 1885, Chinese immigrants—with the exception of teachers, scientists, clergymen and their families, and merchants and their families—were charged a head tax of $50 before admittance into Canada, and this was increased to $100 in 1901 and to $500 in 1904.[86]

In spite of the immensely difficult terrain, construction on Onderdonk's section of the rail line progressed rapidly, and by late 1882, he was persuaded to take over the construction of two more sections, the first from Port Moody, located at the head of Burrard Inlet, to Emory Bar, the second from Savona's Ferry to Craigellachie in Eagle Pass. By the summer of 1884, the rail line was completed from Port Moody to the settlement of Ashcroft, and now, instead of construction materials coming upriver by boat to Yale and then being hauled all the way to the construction site by freight wagon or pack train, they could be brought as far as Ashcroft by work train. Onderdonk immediately moved his head-quarters there, too, and all the freighting companies followed him.

With the pounding of the last spike at Craigellachie in November 1885, Ashcroft superseded Yale as the transportation hub for the Cariboo since freight could now be shipped by rail from both eastern Canada and the west coast for forwarding there. It became even more convenient after 1886, when a bridge was constructed over the Thompson River linking the town with the Cariboo Road. By the end of that year, Barnard's Express Company (generally known as the BX) had also moved its headquarters from Yale to Ashcroft. It was followed there by Oliver Harvey and Bill Bailey, Onderdonk's former bookkeepers, who had joined forces to establish a new business, the Harvey Bailey Company. From their new warehouse near the Canadian Pacific Railway station in Ashcroft, they contracted with the owners of freight wagons and pack trains to move goods all over the Cariboo. More new businesses grew up around them, and the *BC Directory* shows that by 1887 approximately a hundred people were living in Ashcroft, and eighty structures—warehouses, general stores, blacksmith shops, harness and wheel repair shops, livery stables, hotels, bars and homes—had been built there.[87] Yale, which had been the biggest city west of Chicago and north of San Francisco, shrank to little more than a village.

Cataline, like all the other packers who had been contracting for Onderdonk out of Yale, had moved his base north to Ashcroft in 1884, and he stayed on there after the rail line was finished since there was now plenty of freight coming in on the railway from both east and west that was destined for points north. Virginia Bell recalled her grandfather, William B.V. Bailey of the Harvey Bailey Company, telling her that Cataline had driven "supplies out of Ashcroft"[88] for him at that time. As forwarding agents, the company inevitably developed a special relationship with all the freight wagon owners and horse and mule train packers working out of Ashcroft, operating as their message centre and sometimes as a

Caux's Pack Train loading at Harvey Baileys for Babine Lake–1897

In 1884, Cataline relocated his base from Yale to Ashcroft, and he began working closely with the Harvey Bailey Company, a relationship that proved mutually beneficial. Image 411 courtesy of the Kamloops Museum & Archives

bank for them, because while they were on the trail, they had no access to banks, stores or post offices. Cataline, more than any of the others, relied on these services because of his difficulties with language and writing.

While most of the packers working out of Ashcroft in these years wintered their animals in the Bonaparte Valley because it was close to the railway and to a ready supply of grain, Cataline continued to winter his horses and mules on the river flats at Dog Creek south of Williams Lake, because the "old pack trail" went right through the community, making it easily accessible.

Hilary Place's grandfather, Joseph Smith Place, a carpenter and storekeeper, arrived in Dog Creek in the early 1880s, and he described the area at that time as

> a thriving settlement of several hundred peo-
> ple. There were three large stores, four hotels, a
> dance hall, two houses of ill repute and cabins
> all over the place from the River Ranch to Rab-
> bit Park. Remember that at this time there was
> not much at Vancouver, which [was not incor-
> porated until 1886].[89]

Cataline never pre-empted land at Dog Creek, but it was accepted locally that he was the owner of the field where his animals spent the winter each year. In fact, in the winter of 1884–85, when the people of Dog Creek petitioned the government for mail service to be increased from every two weeks to every week, he was asked to sign the petition since he was considered a resident of the community. At first, he may have boarded at the River Ranch owned by Joseph and Jane Place or at Pigeon's Grandview Ranch,[90] but in time he built his own small cabin near the Cornwall brothers' ranch at Ashcroft. It was here that his remarkably tough constitution was noted by his neighbours: he never wore mitts or any covering over his ears, even in sub-zero weather. And all winter long, he would emerge each morning from his cabin stark naked and roll in the snow, rubbing it all over his body and then saying as he went back indoors, "She's good, oui!"[91]

While Cataline was packing for the railway in the 1880s, he began acquiring the crew members who would become intimately connected with his long-term legendary status in the province. In late 1881, he hired a twenty-four-year-old Frenchman born within five miles (eight kilometres) of his own birthplace in Béarn. Joseph Castillou was following in the footsteps of his two older brothers, who had emigrated to the United States a decade earlier. Why he chose to come to British Columbia instead is unknown, but it is possible he had heard the stories told by Jean-Pierre Caux after he returned home to Oloron-Sainte-Marie a decade earlier. Joe Castillou was married, but he had left his wife, Emma Enstrim, behind in Béarn while he became established in this new country. Although he was almost twenty years younger than Cataline—Joe Castillou was born on November 24, 1857, the same year Cataline left France for North America—the two men quickly bonded since they had language, culture and possibly even acquaintances in common. Sometime after Cataline's partnership with Sauveur Buc was dissolved in 1882, Cataline and Castillou became business partners, an arrangement that would last until the early 1890s, when Castillou purchased land in the Nicola Valley, ten miles south of Merritt, to launch his Coldwater Valley Ranch and bring his wife to Canada. His son Henry Castillou, who was born there on May 25, 1896, became famous in BC as a judge and a champion of Indigenous rights as well as an amateur anthropologist and raconteur.[92]

According to Judge Henry Castillou:

> [After 1884 his father, Joseph Castillou, and Cataline had] outfitted out of Ashcroft and packed into different parts of the country, and then as they came down the trail—the old trail went around by Chimney Creek—they left a number of horses at Dog Creek.... The balance of them went into Nicola [where] pack saddles were made [for them]. These old [saddles] were made by hand there in the winter, and in the

> spring the wild ones were driven in and broken
> by just putting bags of sand on [the saddles] and
> throwing the famous double diamond hitch and
> letting them buck themselves out.[93]

Around 1890, Cataline hired a young man named Dave Wiggins, the son of a Líl'wat woman and a black American named Arthur Wiggins, who was reputed to have lived in a cave on the side of Pavilion Mountain. The elder Wiggins was arrested in July 1860 on a charge of "giving squaws whiskey and fined £10 or in default two months on the chain gang."[94] Dave was born around 1871–72 so would have been in his late teens when he went to work for Cataline, but he seems to have already been a seasoned packer, and Cataline soon promoted him to *segundo*.

In those days, Cataline still maintained the habit of carrying trade goods whenever he was contracted to take a load of goods north, and his pack train would stop at Indigenous villages, independent trading posts and mining camps along the route in order to make sales. There was ritual in these transactions, especially when they stopped at Indigenous settlements. Joe Castillou told his son that

> when Cataline—or Jean Caux—commenced
> trading, Dave would put together a chair made
> out of birch and rawhide. Jean Caux would start
> to trade with the famous Nahanni chief. He
> would dress for the occasion. He had a boiled
> shirt, which had been on his back all the way
> from Ashcroft, and Dave would supply a collar,
> yellow with age, a high collar and a little tie,
> not too clean, and he had a French hat. It's not
> that round Christy-stiff hat that we know, but it

was an oval hat that folded. It had been folded for so long that all the hairs running straight down had broken off and it was just the hairs that were running round that were any good, and Dave would paste them back carefully each time it was used so that the hair... the threads, rather, not the hair, the threads running round the hat would be intact when they opened the fold again. He had an old morning coat, green with age. He always wore a big bucking-belt, about ten inches wide with little buckles all the way down, and the Indians called them his corsets. Around this morning coat, green with age, he had a red French-Canadian wool sash, and these black mackinaw pants and moccasins, and he sat in the chair.

All of us great unwashed, we sat on the ground. The Nahanni chief, he took a $10 bill and he lighted the $10 bill, and Cataline always carried big cigars. He just smoked a cigar on state occasions. Before the great trading started the Nahanni chief put a $10 bill in the fire and lighted Cataline's cigar and let the $10 bill burn in the presence of all the assorted gathering. Friendship is greater than wealth. And the trading started. Once the trading started, of course, all the rules were barred.

When the pack train stopped in white settlements, a crowd always gathered.

Cataline would grab these 100-lb sacks and whip them onto the pack train with his *segundo*, Dave Wiggins, on the other side, and all the cheechakos coming up the road would watch these proceedings, you see. They'd say, "My, what a strong man you are, Cataline!" and Cataline said, "That's nothing. My partner, he lift a horse!" Now this was a trained stunt. The little white mare that led the mules weighed about 450 pounds... [it was] very small—a cayuse. They'd trained her that when [Joe Castillou] put his arms round her four legs, she would fold and he'd just lift her off the ground. So Cataline said, "That's nothing. I got the man here, my partner, Joe Castillou, he lift a horse!"

"Oh, no, no," they said, "no man can lift a horse."

So [they would bet] a bottle of cognac that his partner [could not] lift a horse. So they'd bring in the little bell mare, and [Joe] would put his arms around the four legs and just lift the little mare about three inches off the ground. So they started off always [with] a bottle of cognac—it never failed—and the famous bartender, Jimmy Veasey, he arranged always to get some famous travelling dude to supply the bottle. Then they'd proceed up the famous Cariboo Road, famed both in song and story, and on and on into the wilderness.[95]

In 1894, Cataline acquired another employee who would become part of his legend, a Chinese man named Ah Gun, newly arrived in the country. He had been born in China in 1870, so he was just twenty-four when he began working for Cataline, and although the 1901 census lists him as a cook, he soon took on the role of *cargador* for Cataline.

⚬━⚬

With Ashcroft as the new distribution centre for the north and the road network throughout the Cariboo improving year by year, by the 1890s there were literally hundreds of covered freight wagons pulled by teams of horses or oxen on the roads, taking work from the pack trains. The Harvey Bailey Company of Ashcroft had at least seventy-five freight wagons on the road, some of them capable of hauling as many as 18,000 pounds (8165 kilograms) of goods.[96] Packers were reduced to taking whatever work they could get, most of it being in the off-road areas where wagons could not travel.

Fortunately for Cataline, his reputation for reliability meant that he could still count on regular contracts with the Hudson's Bay Company to pack goods to their fur-trade posts in New Caledonia. His annual routine now began as soon as the snow melted in the spring. He brought his mules from their winter quarters in Dog Creek to Ashcroft to load up with provisions and begin their first trip of the season to Quesnel, going on from there to Fort Fraser, Fort St. James and Fort McLeod, returning to Quesnel several weeks later with furs. He made several of these round trips for the company each summer, but in the late summer of 1892, he arrived back at Dog Creek from his final trip of the season to discover that two Englishmen had filed for a pre-emption on the plot of land adjoining what he considered his homestead—although he had

Cataline did many summertime round trips collecting furs for the Hudson's Bay Company in Quesnel, while the rest of the packing industry were forced to find new work as roads north of Ashcroft became more accessible to freight wagons. Image 5975.82.1 courtesy of the Quesnel & District Museum and Archives

apparently never filed a pre-emption—and they had diverted the creek that irrigated his hayfield, leaving him with no hay to winter his mules. According to legend:

> Wrathfully, he called upon the homesteaders and threatened to shoot them if they didn't blow out their dam. The Englishmen put up little argument, but they proceeded to lay a complaint against Cataline, charging that they had complied with the law, staked their water rights and paid their fees. They asked that Cataline be put under bond to keep the peace.

The constable, who knew Cataline well, went out to talk it over with him but found him unreasonable in the extreme. He then summonsed him to appear in court before Judge Begbie. The judge, having known Cataline for these many years, looked rather leniently on his case and, as the creek had ample water for all, decided that the Englishmen should allow half the water to go to Cataline.

Before closing the case, the judge lectured Cataline severely, admonishing him: "In future, you must pay your taxes [and] your water rights, and live up to the letter of the law. What would you have done," he asked, "had I awarded the Englishmen all of the water rights?"

Cataline… [drew] forth a long, shining knife. His black eyes looking straight at the judge, he replied succinctly, "Killa de judge!"[97]

CATALINE'S MEXICAN KNIFE

Sperry Cline told the story of Cataline's Mexican knife:

> Cataline's most prized possession was his knife. Although I never did get a chance to examine it closely, I believe it was the type that Mexicans use for throwing. All through his eventful career he kept it within reach. In the day it was in his bootleg, at night it was under his pillow. There were several stories of his having used it to discourage aggressors, but only one instance came to my knowledge.
>
> A party of young bloods from the outside world visiting Hazelton were endeavouring to show the local hillbillies what life was like in a more sophisticated community. Cataline was in the bar when this crowd was displaying its talents, and they decided to have some fun with the old codger. After a while the old man thought they had gone far enough. He went over to the other side of the room and examined a spot on the wall about the size of a 50-cent piece. He made such a display of the examination that it attracted everybody's attention.
>
> Then he backed away 12 or 15 feet, drew his knife from his boot and made a perfect bullseye. He quickly retrieved the knife, turned to his tormentors and said: "Sacreedam—dat all I tella you now."
>
> It was enough. The bantering abruptly stopped.[98]

THE YUKON
FIELD FORCE

Although the arrival of the CPR in 1886 had brought an economic boom to British Columbia, the railway had also made the province vulnerable to the economic fluctuations of the outside world. In 1893, a continent-wide financial collapse occurred, beginning in the United States with the price of wheat crashing and ending with bank failures and railway bankruptcies. Soon every sector of the economy on both sides of the international border was affected. In BC, which was largely dependent on the sale of lumber, minerals and farm products, jobs vanished and soup kitchens were established in the cities to feed the destitute.

During these years, freighting jobs were scarce, and Cataline was happy to accept any that were offered by mining companies, both in the Cariboo and Omineca, although they were no longer the small placer outfits of his early packing days. Instead, these companies were extracting the gold from deep diggings with enormous dredging machines that had been brought as far north by road as possible, then moved the rest of the way in pieces by pack train. In 1895–96, Cataline made several packing trips to the Bullion Mine in Quesnel Forks and the Horsefly Hydraulic Mine, and in 1898, his mules pulled the first wagon from the end of the road at Quesnel all the way to a mining camp at Manson Creek, a distance of 267 miles (430 kilometres). The mules, being extremely trail-wise, adapted to "the wheels and running gear all right, but the tongue [of the wagon] had to be cut in two."[99] Cataline's friend Sperry Cline recalled that contracts of this kind were

> a new adventure in packing, and no one could estimate the costs with any real degree of accuracy. Cataline took the contract, having been financed by the bank at Quesnel. He ran into a great deal of difficulty in the first two years, and the bank now found that he was some $20,000 in arrears—a lot of money in those days. He was called to the bank and the manager explained the situation. After a lengthy discourse the banker said, "Cataline, we do not doubt your honesty or ability, but we do think you are very careless." Cataline pondered this for a moment before he said, "I thinka da bank dam careless, too." Later things took a turn for the better and he made good the deficit.[100]

In June 1898, Cataline and his pack train were hired by the Hudson's Bay Company to take supplies north from Telegraph Creek to the Yukon for the newly created Yukon Field Force. Almost two years earlier, gold had been discovered on a tributary of the Klondike River, and by the summer of 1898, as many as 25,000 prospectors and adventurers had entered the Yukon, all intent on making their fortunes. About 80 per cent of them were Americans, however, and since their presence was seen as a threat to the territory's sovereignty, the Dominion government had organized

In 1898, Cataline delivered supplies to the newly created Yukon Field Force (shown above), a contingent of the North-West Mounted Police instated to police the perceived threat of American prospectors flooding into the area during the Klondike gold rush. Image C-001338 courtesy of Library and Archives Canada

military reinforcements for the small contingent of North-West Mounted Police (NWMP) that had been policing the Yukon since 1894. The Yukon Field Force that set out by train from Ottawa in the spring of 1898 included 133 men from the Royal Regiment of Canadian Infantry, 16 Royal Canadian Dragoons, 49 men from the Royal Canadian Artillery and 5 staff; they were commanded by Lieutenant-Colonel Thomas Dixon Byron Evans of the Dragoons. In Vancouver, before boarding the SS *Islander* for Wrangell, they were joined by four nurses, a NWMP chaperone, and Alice Freeman, a pioneer woman reporter who wrote for the *Toronto Globe* as "Faith Fenton."

They arrived in Wrangell on May 16, travelled up the Stikine River on the Hudson's Bay Company steamer *Strathcona*, and reached Glenora Landing in early June, twelve miles (nineteen kilometres) downstream from Telegraph Creek. There the army unloaded their supplies, which weighed—depending on the information source—a total of sixty[101] or one hundred[102] tons (fifty-four or ninety tonnes). From that point, the troops were to march north over a brand-new, approximately 130-mile (209-kilometre) trail to the foot of Teslin Lake, accompanied by mule trains relaying the bulk of their supplies. At Teslin Lake, they would load the supplies aboard boats to complete the journey to their new base of operations at Fort Selkirk, located at the confluence of the Yukon and Pelly Rivers.

To make the packing leg of this expedition from Telegraph Creek to Teslin Lake possible, the Dominion government had contracted the Hudson's Bay Company to provide 300 mules and all the necessary packers. Unfortunately, in June 1898, when the field force finally arrived at Glenora Landing, they discovered that only 141 mules and their crews had been assembled there to do the job. Obviously, someone in the company had not done the job properly, and Fenton, indignant at this mismanagement, told her readers in her next *Globe* dispatch that

> there is no doubt whatever that the Hudson
> Bay Company, by reason, doubtless, of ineffi-
> cient management on the part of those officials
> to whom the supervision was deputed, failed
> utterly to grasp the necessities of the situation
> or make provision for the same.[103]

It was a full month before enough pack animals and packers were rounded up to do the job, and among them were Cataline, his crew and his sixty mules. This was, of course, very familiar territory to him since Telegraph Creek had been his headquarters when he was packing for the Cassiar gold rush, and it was where his daughter Clemence had been born. However, he had last seen it sixteen years earlier, and the settlement had grown. It now included two general stores, a hotel, two bakeries, a restaurant, two warehouses, a wharf in the process of construction, and about a dozen log houses, although most of the settlement's 350 inhabitants still lived in tents.[104]

The decision to have the Yukon Field Force take this "all-Canadian" route north to the Yukon had been made in the belief that the trail was passable. It had been surveyed by railway men William Mackenzie and Donald Mann for their "Yukon Railway," and they had even begun preliminary work on the roadbed, but a federal bill permitting the construction of the line had died in the Senate that April, and the contractors had immediately stopped work. After their departure, a forest fire had swept through the area, although fortunately recent heavy rains had doused most of it. On June 12, after a party of soldiers from the Yukon Field Force returned from reconnoitering the route's condition, Private Edward Lester, who kept a journal throughout the trip, wrote that

> the wagon road extends for five or six miles [eight or ten kilometres] beyond the camp and was constructed by Messrs. Mackenzie and Mann. The work for some reason is now at a standstill and consequently the remainder of the road to Teslin Lake is simply an Indian trail.

This is reported to be in fairly good condition
as far as the Tahltan River (25–30 miles) [40–
48 kilometres]. I hear it is pretty tough after.
However, I suppose we shall get there somehow.
There is, I believe, a party of ax-men to be se-
lected from all Companies who are to set out
at once and push right on to Teslin; they are to
bridge a "corduroy" when necessary.[105]

Meanwhile, the government had been widely advertising this
all-Canadian route to the Yukon—Ashcroft to Quesnel to Hazelton
to Telegraph Creek to Teslin Lake—to would-be prospectors so
that when the first unit of the Yukon Field Force finally set out for
Teslin Lake in late June, the trail had already been "broken in" by
a small army of prospectors on foot as well as by a couple of herds
of cattle. It rained for the first week of the field force's journey, and
they made no more than eight miles (thirteen kilometres) a day, and
after the skies cleared, they found themselves in the remains of the
forest fire. Then they stumbled through bogs overlaying perma-
frost, "through forests and over swamps, but everywhere there was
mud, in many places halfway up to [their] knees, and [they] were
unable to do more than two or two and a half miles an hour,"[106]
all the time fighting off swarms of mosquitoes and flies. It took
a month for each pack train to reach Teslin Lake and return to
Telegraph Creek for another load, and all of the supplies had to be
delivered by a freeze-up date of August 31. Private Lester, who was
with the second company of the field force to set out on the trail,
summarized the troop's adventures in the final pages of his journal.

Sometimes our way lay for miles and miles
through blackened smoking trees and over bogs

yet licked by tongues of flame, tracing the trail as best we could over the hot, smoking ashes whilst the crash of falling trees added to the intensity of the situation.... Alternating with all this came spells of bog travelling, which is a more serious matter, at all events from a packer's point of view. This "soft land" begins in real earnest about 40 or 50 miles [64 or 80 kilometres] south of Teslin [Lake] intersected here and there by ridges of solid ground. Gazing round from a vantage point on one of these ridges, we see on either side of us, as far as the eye can reach, nothing but low-lying bog... of varying degrees of stability. This wet swampy ground almost invariably centres to a perfect slough of despond in which our pack mules sink to their girths... this bog is not necessarily confined to low-lying land but rather it belongs to the hills.

A great deal of corduroying has been done and stretches of over a quarter mile [402 metres] bridge many of the soft spots, but this corduroy is not long-lasting. We experienced many instances of corduroy laid early in the season, perhaps by inexperienced hands. The bog had worked into deep holes at either end, the logs had shifted and huge gaps formed in the surface, and this with the loose shifting logs rendered the whole thing highly dangerous both to man and beast, and in many places it

had been flung aside by desperate packers who
preferred braving the dangers of the boggy spot
to risking their animals' legs on the obnoxious
corduroy.[107]

By 1898, Cataline had been packing for forty years and had
a reputation as one of the best in the business, partly because the
welfare of his crew and his animals was always paramount for
him. However, the conditions on the Telegraph Creek-Teslin Lake
trail were probably worse than any he and his men had encoun-
tered before, with mules constantly mired in the mud and meeting
with accidents. As well, he clashed with the commander of the
field force, Lieutenant-Colonel Evans of the Dragoons, a rather
pompous man who insisted on everything being done according
to military rules, even in these trying conditions. The colonel, in
turn, did not appreciate Cataline calling him "Boy," especially in
front of his troops. Their most celebrated clash became a legend
that was retold in many forms over the years, although the gist of
the story was always the same. The following is the version told by
Cataline's friend Sperry Cline.

> Cataline complained about the army's incessant
> blowing of bugles as it upset his animals. "Alla
> time blowa de buga, scara de mule, no gooda."
> He was most unhappy about the bugles in the
> morning when he was trying to gentle his mules
> into their workday and get them loaded....
> One day a mule fell, rolled on top of its pack
> and became helpless. Several of the soldiers
> attempted the rescue but, never having mas-
> tered the intricacies of the diamond hitch, were

soon hopelessly involved. The O.C. came up and took charge of the situation but only succeeded in making matters worse. When he had exhausted his few ideas, he looked around and saw that Cataline had ridden up and had been quietly watching his efforts. He swallowed his pride and appealed for help.... Cataline, with a touch of triumph in his voice, replied, "Blowa da buga, Boy! Blowa da buga!"[108]

In spite of the delay at the beginning of the project, packing the field force's supplies to the foot of Teslin Lake was completed by early August, and the soldiers continued north in a convoy of five pilot boats and four scows, rowing by day and camping on shore by night, so that they reached Fort Selkirk on September 11. The pack trains returned to Telegraph Creek as they had come. Meanwhile, the government ordered the Hudson's Bay Company to sell the mules bought especially for this venture in order to avoid paying for their winter feed. Cataline and his mules began the long march south; he would winter them at Dog Creek before journeying on to Ashcroft.

⊶⊷

In the spring of 1899, Cataline had the pleasure of being in demand for two packing jobs, the first being from Colonel Wright, who for a number of years had packed the mail north from Ashcroft. By this time, Quesnel's mail was leaving Ashcroft every Monday and Friday morning, and now a new mail service would take the mail on from there to Stuart Lake and Manson Creek once a month.[109] This was an area that Cataline now knew almost as well as he knew the back of his hand, so it was Wright's contract he accepted.

The second contract offer had come from the Hudson's Bay Company, asking him to pack goods from Hazelton to Manson Creek, but since he knew the story behind that offer, he was not eager to become involved in it. In 1866, the company had established a small fort at Hazelton because of its convenient position at the head of navigation on the Skeena River, but they had closed it ~~again~~ within a few years, because it had not produced the profit they expected. They had reopened it in 1880, however, in order to use it as a base for bringing in some of the annual supplies for the company's New Caledonia forts, including at least seventy tons (sixty-four tonnes) of flour and all manner of dry goods and mining equipment. The problem with this route was the repeated loading and unloading of cargo that was necessary, because it all had to be transported down Babine Lake in canoes, then packed across the nine-mile (fourteen-kilometre) Babine Portage to Stuart Lake to be loaded aboard canoes again for the journey south to Fort St. James, located at the foot of the lake. Furs were shipped out by the reverse route.

In 1893, the company had improved on the system by replacing the canoes with York-type schooners, but it was still a difficult journey. As a result, company executives had become convinced that it was time to get completely out of the packing business, and they had arranged the sale of their Fort St. James pack train to the partnership of George Adolphus Veith and Robert Borland. These two men ran a cattle ranch at 150 Mile House and had for a number of years been driving cattle and packing flour north from the mill at Soda Creek to the Hudson's Bay Company forts in New Caledonia. Having been happily rid of their last animals, the company had given Veith and Borland the contract to carry all of the company's goods on the Hazelton-Fort McLeod route.

Unfortunately, in 1898, Veith and Borland had sold off their pack animals to the North-West Mounted Police, and the Hudson's Bay Company was forced to go back into the packing business. The company subsequently purchased another seventy mules and a bell mare from Walla Walla in Washington State and from the Cariboo Hydraulic Mining Company,[110] staked off two quarter-sections of land in the Bulkley Valley, fifty-five miles (eighty kilometres) southeast of Hazelton, cleared land for a hay meadow and built shelters for the mules. Then they began looking for a new contractor. But packers were in short supply since this was now the height of the Klondike gold rush, and when Cataline turned the job down, the company was forced to operate the pack train itself.

At the same time, the Hudson's Bay Company had begun searching for a new contractor for their Ashcroft-to-Quesnel-to-Fraser Lake packing route. While they required packers every year for each of their supply routes, they never knew exactly how many animals per route would be needed until the incoming freight was sorted and packed and they had determined its dimensions and weight. They also delayed setting the rate they would offer until close to departure time, hoping that other companies would be offering a lower rate that season and they would then only have to match that rate. But this could backfire, since there were just so many good packers available, and if they delayed too long, they would have to hire men who were unreliable or drunk or broke or all three. Packers, on the other hand, delayed committing to the job, hoping to be offered a better rate from some other shipper in order to make this difficult and insecure way of life at least lucrative.

The men of the Hudson's Bay Company were, however, shrewd negotiators, accustomed to playing one packer off against another, always encouraging competition in order to get better packing prices, and they intended to do so even in these circumstances. That year, therefore, they looked for a packer who was willing to take on a company chattel mortgage as well. As one of the fur trade supervisors explained very reasonably:

> In giving us a Bill of Sale of their pack train, the parties no doubt fully understand that the Company, in obtaining this from them, do so in order to get absolute protection, and if they treat us fairly, they may rest satisfied that no unfair advantage will be taken of them.[111]

Arrangements of this kind had been known to miscarry for the company, and this was certainly the case with their next contractors, Ignacio Sanchez and his partner, Joseph Aguayo. Both had been born in Mexico, and Sanchez was one of the packers who had entered British Columbia at the time of the Fraser River gold rush. But he was now about seventy years old and very ill (he died later that year), so Aguayo was left with the responsibility of fulfilling the contract. The results were disastrous, and on November 3, 1898, A.C. McNabb at the Hudson's Bay Company's post in Quesnel received word from Fraser Lake that Aguayo had only reached that post with the pack train the previous day. Writing to Robert H. Hall, who managed the fur trade in BC from the company's headquarters in Victoria, McNabb explained he had been advised that

> both the pack and train were in bad condition. Aguayo left here on the 17th of October, and was therefore 16 days in reaching Fraser Lake owing as he says to his horses having strayed. The season is now late, snow having fallen,

that I think it is extremely doubtful if he will reach Quesnel with the horses alive. This man has proved by his work this season that he is not capable of doing packing. Steps should be taken to [secure] whatever is left of the train when he reaches Meldrums [Creek] with them, and some settlement made with him for his summer's work.... He will never clear the [debt with us], and the only way to do so is for the company to take over the train and work it ourselves.[112]

Aguayo was fired and the Hudson's Bay Company seized the pack train. Meanwhile, in the spring of 1899, Hall had also begun looking for a new packer to take over their Hazelton to Manson's Creek route, a distance of 180 miles (290 kilometres). As Hall explained to Boyd in Quesnel:

The rate we propose to pay this season... at 9¢ is a very high price for the distance on a good pack trail, and there should be good money in it if [the new contractors] have pack animals which can carry average loads. The great trouble with many packers is the small average which their animals can carry.... A pack train reaching Hazelton in good time should make four full trips [per year] to the Omineca, and even if they only averaged 250 lbs. [113 kg] to the pack, the animals would earn $90 per head for the season.[113]

Hall had then appealed to W.B. Bailey, the storage and for-warding agent in Ashcroft, for help finding the right man for the job. (Bailey was happy to oblige since services of this kind main-tained good relations with the Hudson's Bay Company and kept the packing industry running smoothly.) Cataline was at the top of Bailey's list, but he had already accepted Wright's contract, so the company offered the job to the partnership of Tierney and Cleve-land, who had spent the previous three seasons engaged in mining and packing. There were two problems with giving the contract to these men: first, their present pack train consisted of just twenty animals with no "rigging," so they required an advance of $400 to purchase more mules and equipment. Second, according to a letter written by the company's man in Quesnel on April 22, 1899: "I cannot say that neither Tierney or his partner drink as both do, and the partner is liable to get on a spree every time he gets to a place where he can get liquor, but in all other respects is a reliable man."[114] In fact, Tierney and Cleveland only lasted one season as packers for the company because they "behaved scandalously,"[115] and in the winter of 1899–1900, the company began the search once again for reliable packers. Hall laid out his requirements as "a first-class sober and honest head packer and four assistant packers for which I am prepared to pay $100 and $50 each per month."[116] As this time, the company would not have to compete with what Hall described as the "Klondike excitement" in their quest for packers—they would only have to pay what he consid-ered "fair wages in return for fair services and no more."[117] But instead of a gold rush, this time the company had to compete with a telegraph line.

THE YUKON
TELEGRAPH LINE

⌐═✦═⌐

The events of the Klondike Gold Rush had made it clear that much better communication with the north was needed to protect Canada's sovereignty, and in March 1899, the Dominion Government Telegraph Service (DGTS) announced that a line would be built to the Yukon. The Dominion government had already refurbished the section of the old Collins telegraph line that had been built between Ashcroft and Quesnel, and it had subsequently been leased to the CPR, guaranteeing timely communication between the Cariboo and the Lower Mainland. The next step in establishing a link with the Yukon was stringing a line from Dawson City to Bennett on the BC-Yukon border, and this was completed on September 28, 1899.[118]

In March 1900, Jean Baptiste Charleson, the DGTS's construction supervisor for the new line, set four crews to work building the Quesnel to Bennett section of the line, a distance of approximately 1000 miles (1600 kilometres); the goal was to have it finished by October, when winter conditions would halt construction. The task of the work crews was to clear a twelve-foot-wide (3.65 metres) right-of-way through forests, over rivers and streams, and up and down mountains, dig post holes, and erect twenty-foot-tall (six-metre) poles or top living trees to carry the cable. Every thirty or forty miles (forty-eight or sixty kilometres) the crews were also to construct a log cabin big enough to house a lineman and a telegrapher as well as smaller refuge huts between the cabins. The first crew worked south from Bennett towards Atlin in northern British Columbia. Crew number two worked south from Atlin to meet crew number three working north from Hazelton. This was the most difficult section because the terrain was extremely rugged and much of it was also heavily timbered. Crew number four worked north from Quesnel, cutting costs wherever possible by using Indigenous trails and the long-abandoned Collins Telegraph Line right-of-way.

The project required thousands of pounds of heavy-duty galvanized cable; thousands of porcelain insulators and the oak brackets used to mount them on the poles; kegs of nails; all the windows, stoves and other furnishings necessary for the line cabins; as well as tools and provisions for the workmen. All of it was taken by steamboat to Hazelton or Telegraph Creek or by freight wagon from Ashcroft to Quesnel, but the only way to get it from these distribution points to the worksites was via pack train, and as the line progressed, the pack train trips got longer and longer—some of them as long as 100 miles (160 kilometres). As a result, there was work for every packer in the province who was willing to endure the mud, mosquitoes and blackflies. In order to pay all the freighting and labour costs associated with the local workers in a timely manner, the federal government signed an agreement with the Hudson's Bay Company for the company's Fort St. James post to act as paymaster.

Cataline and the sixty-mule train that he operated out of Ashcroft were contracted to work on the section of the line that lay between Quesnel and Hazelton, and after it was finished on schedule in the fall of 1900, he delivered provisions to the linemen's cabins along that sector. Guy Lawrence, author of the book *40 Years on the Yukon Telegraph* (published by Mitchell Press in 1965), met him on the trail that summer, and his memories of that meeting were not altogether happy ones. In a letter to the editor of the *British Columbia Digest*, Lawrence wrote:

> Our first meeting was not a very friendly one, and occurred when his train of some 57 mules and horses was packing supplies for the Yukon Telegraph Service. I was at Blackwater [west of Quesnel] at the time, and with my lineman, George Duclos, we ran a bunkhouse and stable for those travelling up and down the Blackwater Road from Quesnel to the Nazko Valley. It happened that we had a quarter section of land a mile from the station at Blackwater which contained a natural meadow and which we had planted in redtop. We had cut the hay and stacked it, and carefully built a pole fence around the stack. When Cataline's pack train delivered the annual supplies, the Chinaman in charge of the train removed the fence around the stack, with the result that about six tons of hay was either eaten or badly trampled on by the stock. Cataline and I had a long argument, which finally ended in a couple of shots of rum and a promise that I would later receive restitution. However, the old man must have forgotten his promise.[119]

Alice Northcott Earley, Quesnel's telegraph operator from 1891 to 1903, had better memories of her meeting with Cataline that summer.

> That was a busy time for they were building the Yukon Telegraph line…. It was quite a sight to watch [Cataline's] pack mules cross the Fraser River. Billy Bouchie would ferry their… pack harnesses across in the canoe and arrange them along the road on the other side. Then Cataline would ride over and hold the bell mare's halter so she swam behind, and he'd jingle her bell all the way. Those mules would fall over themselves to jump in and swim after her. When they got across, every mule would go to his own pack and stand ready for it to be put on his back.
>
> I remember one time watching the pack train head north across the river—all except one mule. For some reason he decided he didn't want to go. He lay down and nothing the men could do would move him—until one [of the crew] ran down to the river and filled his hat with water. Then he poured the water into the mule's ear. You should have seen that mule jump to his feet and streak up the trail. His tail stood out straight. The two packers were rocking with laughter.[120]

Before the first snow fell in 1900, Cataline had time to take on a few more contracts in the north, and one of them was packing an electric light plant from Quesnel to the 43rd Mining & Milling

Company's gold-mining operation at Dunkeld on Manson Creek in the Omineca district. According to legend,

> Cataline loaded the engine base, which weighed 560 pounds, onto the toughest and most ornery mule in his train, old "Sundaygait," [which] stood seventeen and a half hands [high].
>
> But Sundaygait knew his business when it came to packing heavy loads. A platform was built across the *aparejo* and, from a specially-built tripod, the engine base was lowered by means of a set of blocks onto [the *aparejo* on] Sundaygait's back. The tripod and tackle were carried on a service mule led close behind [so the lighting plant could be loaded and unloaded each day].... Three weeks after leaving Quesnel Cataline unloaded the engine base at the 43rd's workings at Dunkeld on Kildare Gulch. Sundaygait, relieved of his load [for the final time], stretched his long length on the ground and lay there for 48 hours straight.[121]

According to the version of this story told by writer Guy Lawrence, Cataline built a stretcher between two mules to carry a lighting plant weighing 650 pounds (295 kilograms).[122]

When winter descended on the north in 1900, there was still a 121-mile (195-kilometre) gap between the workers going south from Atlin and those coming north from Hazelton, forcing both crews to return once the snow melted the following spring. The final hookup was not made until 4:00 p.m. on September 24, 1901, linking Dawson City with Vancouver and the rest of the world.

At an unmarked spot between the fifth and sixth line cabin some 120 miles (194 kilometres) north of Hazelton, Cataline's friend George Biernes, who was in charge of the last pack train, produced the bottle of brandy he had saved to celebrate the occasion. Then, before the men gathered up their gear to begin hiking back to Hazelton, they shot the horses and mules that were not fit enough to make the journey out; the remaining twenty-three animals died on the trip.[123]

The original budget for the line was $225,000; the final bill was more than twice that amount.[124]

⟜

In November 1901, Cataline completed negotiations to buy the Hudson's Bay Company's last pack train, the forty-six mules, six horses and one bell mare the company had been operating from the Bulkley Valley farm to carry goods from Hazelton to Omineca. It was agreed that he would take over the pack train in Hazelton on May 28, 1902, and work off the purchase price at $1000 per year[125] by carrying the company's goods. James Thompson, who had taken over as fur trade superintendent in Victoria from Robert H. Hall, expressed the company's collective relief on the completion of the sale when he wrote that

> the sale of the pack train to Jean Caux on the
> basis arranged will remove a source of much loss
> and worry—besides, conditions have changed
> and there is nothing to be gained now by the
> Company controlling transport of this charac-
> ter at Hazelton.[126]

Although Cataline had packed for the Hudson's Bay Company before, by purchasing the company's pack train with a chattel

An old timer

While stories of the endurance of Cataline's animals vary, horses and mules often carried loads exceeding 500 pounds. Image WP2000-060-2793 courtesy of the Prince Rupert City & Regional Archives

mortgage, he had entered into a very different kind of relationship. Although they would find that he continued to live up to his sterling reputation for an uncanny ability with animals and excellent rapport with his crew, for his reliability in never losing any of the goods entrusted to his pack train and for delivering goods on time, they would soon become totally frustrated with his unique method of doing business. The first indication came in January 1902 when he called on William Bailey of the Harvey Bailey Company in Ashcroft to ask him to write a letter to Thompson. It read:

> Dear Sir,
>
> Mr. Jean (Caw) Cataline has asked us to write and enquire if you will have freight to load about 60 animals from this point for Fraser Lake or Stuart's Lake in April next. He wishes to leave here about the 28th of April as he says he wants to arrive at Hazelton on the 28th of May to take over your pack train at that place.
>
> W. Bailey[127]

Thompson responded that he could give Cataline some freight to take north but not enough to load up sixty animals since most of the company's freight for the north was shipped via Hazelton. Cataline ignored the rebuff and had Bailey write to Thompson again on February 5, 1902.

> Dear Sir,
>
> Mr. Jean Caux has asked us to write to you and request that you kindly advance his daughter, Miss Clemence Caux, the sum of forty dollars

($40) on his account. The young woman will call on you for the amount if you will advance same.

Jean Caux requests that you have whatever freight you can give him for interior points, north of Quesnelle, here by the 15th of April, as he wishes to leave with his train not later than the 28th of that month.[128]

Within days, Thompson, although probably somewhat bemused, responded that Clemence would receive the money "as soon as she makes application for it." He also offered to "give Caux as much as he can take from Ashcroft to Stuart's Lake, say 18,000 pounds [8164 kilograms], provided he will accept same at 8¢ a pound."[129] Cataline kept Thompson waiting a week for his response, which Bailey then sent by telegraph: "Jean Caux accepts your offer. Wants about sixteen thousand pounds."[130]

That spring, when other packers applied to Thompson for contract work, he turned them down, even when they had served the company well in the past; he had to make sure that Cataline got enough work to be able to honour the sale agreement since the company definitely did not want that pack train back again. The *Ashcroft Journal* reported on Saturday, April 25, 1903, that

Cataline started out with his pack train on Wednesday. He takes a cargo to Stuart's Lake for the Hudson's Bay Company and will pack in the North for that company the balance of the season. The weather still keeps cold and he expects the feed very short for a time.

A Plea from Clemence

On February 13, 1902, Clemence wrote a letter from Victoria to her father in Ashcroft. Just seven months earlier, on July 16, 1901, she had given birth to a son, Frederick Allfield Harris. The baby's father was Hugh Allfield Harris, a twenty-nine-year-old American teamster, to whom she was not married, quite possibly because he was already married in the United States. It is also possible that he is "the other party" referred to in her letter.

My Dear Papa,

Mr. Bailey's letter reached me all right. I was very much pleased to hear from you after such a long absence. I hope that it will not occur again, even when you are off to work, for it gives me great pleasure to hear from you and to know that you are well. I went to see Mr. Thompson last Thursday and received the forty dollars without any trouble, he was telling me that he was up to that part of the country last summer and saw you and that you were in very good health. He gave me to understand that you would be working for the Hudson Bay again this season, he thought you would be able to begin work a little after the first of March. I thank you ever so much for the money. Well, Papa, I think I shall get some of that money as the other party does not want it to go to court. I shall try to get my photo taken and send you one, to see if I have changed. Papa, if it is not too much trouble would you please send me one of yours? I have the one you gave me yet. Papa how old are you? We are having fair weather now the snow has all left. Victoria is pretty dull just now. Well, Papa, thank you ever so much for sending me that money and good night for this time.

Your loving daughter,
Clemence G. Caux[131]

However, although company officials were pleased to be out of the packing business and grateful that Cataline was totally reliable, their correspondence with him over the following years—always via a third party—reveals their endless frustration with him, mostly because they found themselves cast in the role of his bankers. But Cataline was only continuing the financial system he had always used: each spring he would set up credit with a bank or the Hudson's Bay Company or the Harvey Bailey Company and then leave it to his customers to pay his creditors or ask his creditors to pay his bills for him. For the most part they did so, although over the years his trusting nature did cost him a great deal of money.

There is an almost comical exchange of letters written in 1904 between Cataline and the company—Cataline's end of the correspondence written by a man named C.F. McDonald—that demonstrates this financial system and reveals the company men's mounting confusion and irritation. Cataline's initial letter was written on January 3, 1904, to Thompson in Victoria.

Dear Sir,

Please give C.F. McDonald the amount of this note which is $83.25 it was due last [August] I have pay it to him and I will make it all right

with you next summer the other notes I gave
[Ferguson] of Hat Creek & McGilvray of
Cache Creek they sent them in last summer
and got credit for them but C.F. McDonald
was under the impression that the note would
not be honoured... he wishes credit for it with
Company's branch in Vancouver.

By so doing
You will oblige
Jean Caux[132]

McDonald added a letter of his own to the packet, then sent
both to the Hudson's Bay Company manager in Vancouver, not to
Thompson in Victoria, and on January 6, that manager sent it on
to Victoria, requesting instructions on what he should do with it.
The reply from Thompson came three days later.

I am surprised to find that the order of 18th
of April last in favor of C.F. McDonald has
not been [paid].... I sent cheques to H.B. Bailey & Company, Ashcroft, for the balance due
to Caux [after the annual $1,000 payment for
the pack train had been taken out], and if they
have not yet been handed over, there may be
a possibility of collecting. I telegraphed Messrs
Bailey this morning to hold McDonald's order
for $83.25 if Caux had not yet been settled with
and will advise you on receipt of a reply.

I may say that this man Caux has given
me more trouble during the past two years

than all the other business of BC District put together. Were it not that he is "working out" the agreed on price of the Company's pack train at Hazelton, I would have nothing to do with him.[133]

When it turned out that Cataline had already been paid for the previous year's packing, Thompson refused to pay McDonald. "It is probable," he wrote back, "that Caux will be packing for the Company again next season, and if so I should endeavor to collect the amount, although I could not give any guarantee." The response he received from Vancouver summed up their joint frustration: "I appreciate your kind attention in this matter and thoroughly recognize what a large amount of trouble and annoyance in business relations with a man such as this must give you."[134]

As time went by, however, the men of the company, having grown accustomed to Cataline's method of doing business, realized his value, and in 1907, when the going rate for moving freight from Hazelton to Babine rose to 4¢, James Thompson wrote to J.C. Boyd, who was now stationed in Hazelton:

Under the circumstances, there is no alternative but to pay that figure for packing the Company's own goods notwithstanding the agreement with Jean Caux. He is under legal obligation to pack at $2\frac{1}{2}$¢, but looking to the future, it would be better to let him see that the Company were prepared to deal fairly with him, and I expect that thereby we will be able to retain his services for the future.[135]

In day-to-day financial transactions that did not involve the Hudson's Bay Company, however, Cataline had no problems. He simply relied on his remarkable memory. Louis LeBourdais, writing in the *Province* newspaper in 1925, retold a story he had heard from Telesphore "Tom" Marion, a Quebecois who operated a general store in Quesnel for thirty years. It seems that two of Cataline's men had quit the train after making a single trip.

> The two men, hired in Quesnel, had gone down with the pack train to Ashcroft, loaded, worked on through to Hazelton and returned to Quesnel again, an interval of three months or more. Cataline brought the packers into Marion's store and from memory called out the items for him to write down on paper… [and he ended with] "So he have coming to him now $147 six bits." Laboriously then, Jean Caux would trace his name on a blank cheque to be filled in by the storekeeper.
>
> The second packer's account was much the same only this man claimed he could "figger" and had kept track of his earnings and expenses in a little book. There was $2 difference between the packer's book and the figures given to Marion by Cataline, and after considerable argument it was discovered that the man had made a mistake in his addition. Cataline was right.
>
> He could neither read nor write but was possessed of a wonderful memory, perhaps from necessity, because being unable to write, he was forced to keep track… of every article

of freight consigned to his care but also to keep account of the men's wages and their expenses on the road; and as he only paid the bills on the return trip, which sometimes covered a period of several months, this was a remarkable feat. [136]

In 1933, LeBourdais penned another story about Cataline's way of doing business for the *Vancouver Sunday Province*'s readers.

Cheques frequently circulated as "cash" for months at a time [in those days]. Occasionally years would pass before they were turned in. Often they bore as many endorsements as there are entries on a present-day blind pig [illegal bar] permit.

Among a fair-sized two-year wad was a cheque returned as "paid" to Stuart Henderson, the criminal lawyer, in 1901.

Henderson's assistant was Fred Calder, now a judge of the County Court of Cariboo. One bright spring morning there [had come] to Calder's home a swarthy, short, broad-shouldered man, dressed in frock coat, white stiff-bosomed shirt, minus collar and tie, and blue denim overalls stuffed into knee-high cowhide boots. His greying black hair hung in wavelets almost to his coat collar. He carried a black toreador hat. It was Jean Caux, familiarily known as Cataline. Crowding 65, or perhaps 70, at that time, he did not look it.... Seated in the front room of Calder's home, Cataline explained that he had come on a matter of business, one that required the services of a lawyer. With difficulty the young Easterner made out what the old packer was driving at, for he spoke a mixture of French, Mexican, Indian and English.

"Oui, but I pay," Cataline insisted, when Calder refused to accept remuneration for his advice. Though fully qualified to hang out his shingle in Nova Scotia, he had no licence in BC, but he realized that it would be futile to try and explain this to Cataline. Besides, he did not feel like taking anything from the picturesque old-timer. He firmly declined to name his fee.

Cataline went away bowing and expressing his thanks. A few months passed, and Cataline came again to see Calder. He proffered at $10 cheque. And in as many languages as he had previously offered his thanks, he steadfastly refused to take it back.

Sorting out his cancelled cheques one day, Henderson came upon one made out to Cataline for $10. In addition to the old packer's mark, it bore the endorsation of F. Calder.

"How is it that you endorsed this cheque?" asked Stuart Henderson, smiling.

"I got it from Cataline," Calder replied, explaining the circumstances.

Whereupon Stuart Henderson—the man who is reputed to have successfully defended more than a score of murder cases as well as numerous other criminal and civil actions—sat on the edge of his desk and laughed.

"He borrowed that money from me, the sly rascal," Henderson explained, "but he didn't tell me that he was going to use it to pay for legal advice obtained from you."[137]

One of Cataline's fervent admirers in these later years of his career was the young fur trader George Ogston, who arrived in Hazelton from Scotland in 1903 to begin working as a Hudson's Bay Company apprentice. Ogston, who remained with the company for the next seven years, wrote:

Cataline might have stepped from the pages of one of Bret Harte's novels, so completely did he fill the bill of what a real western character should look like. Tall, straight, despite his seventy years [Cataline was 65 in 1903], with a magnificent head of hair reaching down to his shoulders in greying curls, he spoke a language which nobody but his mules understood. It seemed to be a curious mixture of Spanish, French, Chinook and Chinese. During the years I knew him, I do not think I ever had a real conversation with him.[138]

THE FINAL
ADVENTURE

◦══✦══◦

After the Yukon Telegraph Line was completed, pack trains were still needed for the provisioning of the linemen's cabins, each of which had to be supplied annually with 3000 to 4000 pounds (1360 to 1814 kilograms) of foodstuffs and other necessities, enough to last the two men stationed there—a telegrapher and a lineman responsible for maintaining the telegraph lines—for the entire year. As had been the case when the telegraph line was under construction, the project was divided into three sections for the provisioning process. The packer who won the Dominion Government Telegraph Service's contract to work out of Quesnel supplied the first five cabins north to Burns Lake, the packer working from Hazelton supplied two cabins to the south and nine to the north, and the packer operating from Telegraph Creek supplied four cabins to the south and three to the north. There was only a short window of opportunity for these provisioning trips; the pack train could not start out before there was sufficient grass on the trail to feed the horses and mules, but all the cabins had to be serviced and the train back at home base before the first snowfall covered the grass again—a period of no more than ten or twelve weeks at most.

Frank Callbreath won the first contract to supply the cabins north and south of Telegraph Creek, while the partnership of Charlie Barrett and Edward "Ned" Charleson, the son of the man who had supervised the construction of the Yukon Telegraph Line, put in the winning bid for the contract to supply the line cabins north and south of Hazelton. Barrett, who owned the Diamond D Cattle Ranch near the junction of the Morice and Bulkley Rivers, was a year-round packer who drove both horse and mule trains in summer and ran dog teams in winter, sometimes as far north as Dawson City.

Due to a mix-up one year, the Barrett-Charleson pack trains returned from their annual provisioning of the cabins north of Hazelton without delivering to cabin #9, the farthest one on the route. It was already late in the season, but Barrett, knowing that the men in that cabin would starve without those supplies, loaded a string of pack horses and set off again on the 170-mile (274-kilometre) trip. He only made it halfway before the trail was blocked by snow, and one by one his horses, unable to forage, began to die off from starvation. Returning to the ranch with his remaining horses, he set off again, this time with a dog team, feeding them en route with the carcasses of the dead horses he had cached on his previous trip. They made it to cabin #9, delivered the provisions and returned to the ranch, although Barrett lost some of his dogs on the way back.

A year or so later, Charleson bowed out of his partnership with Barrett, and in 1907, Cataline bought the contract to provision the Hazelton to Telegraph Creek line of cabins. This was familiar country because he had travelled it during the Cassiar gold rush years and later when going north to carry supplies for the Yukon Field Force. Since November 1901, when he bought the Hudson's Bay Company pack train, he had been operating two trains, using one to take the company's supplies from Ashcroft north to Quesnel and from there to Fort Fraser over a newly improved trail. His *segundo*, Ah (or Joe) Fook, had been taking the second one—the former Hudson's Bay Company pack train—from Hazelton to Fort St. James, although after 1906, some of the supplies on Fook's pack animals were destined for the crews surveying the "mountain division" of the Grand Trunk Pacific Railway's proposed line from Wolf Creek, Alberta, through the Yellowhead Pass to Prince Rupert. (Construction finally began from both ends in May 1908, although the railway was not completed until April 1914.) On the return trip, Fook packed the Hudson's Bay Company's furs to Hazelton. Taking on the telegraph line cabin provisioning contract in addition to the Hudson's Bay Company and Grand Trunk railway contracts meant Cataline had to juggle both crews and animals. One of the deciding factors was the state of the telegraph line trail. The DGTS provided an extra $1000 each year to pay a crew to clear fallen trees and repair bridges before the pack train came through, but even with this advance work, the journey was extremely treacherous—with narrow trails clinging to steep mountainsides, precipices, rock slides and rushing torrents. As a result, Cataline's train for the provisioning trips was composed entirely of mules since they were more sure-footed and could carry more than horses, while his horses were shifted to the Ashcroft-Quesnel-Fort St. James route. However, when winter came, he continued to take all the animals from both pack trains to Dog Creek, packing north again with them in the spring as soon as feed started to grow.[139]

⟜

Cataline's adventures during this last decade of his packing career are more thoroughly documented than those in any of his previous years, partly because there were more people on the roads to note the passage of this legendary man. As well, the Hudson's Bay Company trading posts kept careful note of comings and goings, and in the early years of the twentieth century, every major community had a newspaper with pages to fill.

In 1906, Vital LaForce, a French Canadian prospector, established a cable ferry—a 12- by 20-foot (3.65- by 6.09-metre) scow—across the Nechako River close to Fort Fraser. LaForce's journal records the following pack train transfer for November 5, 1906: "Cataline with 27 horses and 3 men heading for Telegraph Creek."[140]

The turnover in Cataline's crews was constant in these years, because men had more job options as different industries became more prominent. Many young men only hired on as packers for as long as it took them to earn a stake for a homestead or a business, and most of the older men gradually lost the stamina to ride a horse all day and load and unload huge packs. By 1907, Dave Wiggins had moved to Sheep Creek in the Chilcotin to set himself up as a hunting guide. (In February 1929, the *Omineca Herald* reported that "Dave Wiggins was caught supplying liquid refreshments contrary to law to natives and he will not be around for a time."[141]) On the other hand, while Cataline was slowly losing his veteran packers, he was as usual gaining some new young crew members, young fellows in love with the romance of the packer's life. In 1904, a thirteen-year-old Scot named John Ogilvie Davidson hired on as his bellboy. Davidson, who arrived on the job as a "braw lad," developed into a large, brawny packer and acquired the nickname "Skook," short for *skookum*, the Chinook word for strong or powerful. However, according to storyteller Frank Cooke, who professed to have heard the story from Skook himself:

The friendship was put to the test when Skook began eyeing a young Native lady that Cataline had taken a shine to. One day as they were loading up the train, Skook was walking by Cataline when a boot came out and tripped him.

He landed face down and when he rolled over, he found Cataline's knife against his throat. In his buggered up language he got the point across to Skook with words equivalent to "Stay away from her, Scotty, she's my woman." Then for emphasis Cataline moved the knife in an up and down motion that could not be misunderstood. When asked [later] how he dealt with the situation, Skook replied, "I made wide circles around her after that."[142]

Skook Davidson went on to become one of the province's most famous wilderness guides.

Sixteen-year-old Patrick "Paddy" James Carroll was hired in 1907. The young man soon came to idolize Cataline, and in later years, he told his family of the old packer's shrewd humour and hilarious way of expressing himself. One laconic piece of advice he imparted to Carroll was, "Watcha da sterna da mule. Watcha da stemma da monk."[143]

CATALINE FILM

The *Ashcroft Journal* reported on May 1, 1909, that

> Cataline's pack train consisting of some fifty animals left
> town yesterday en route to Stuart's Lake, Fort St. James
> and thence to Hazelton. An interesting feature of their
> departure was the taking of a moving picture by an
> operator sent up by the provincial Department of Ag-
> riculture. The picture will be exhibited in London and
> elsewhere and will doubtless create much interest.[144]

Unfortunately, this film no longer exists. The Royal BC Museum re-
ports that no professional film footage taken of the town of Ashcroft prior
to 1930 has survived.[145]

Cataline's departure from Ashcroft for Hazelton in 1909 was
documented on film, but none of the footage exists today. Image C-09933 courtesy of the Royal BC Museum and Archives

Cataline had a positive effect on several more young lives in his last working years. One was eight-year-old Arthur Baker of Barkerville. Cataline and his pack train had always camped on the Baker family's ranch when they were on their way north or south so that Cataline and Arthur's father, August Baker, could visit over a bottle of whiskey. Their language of choice on these occasions was French since Baker had come from the village of Lafrimbolle in Lorraine. (The original family name was Boulanger, but at some point, it had been changed to Baker.) The boy and his younger sister always ran out to watch as the pack animals were unloaded for the night because there were barrels of whisky, slabs of bacon, sacks of dried beans, and pieces of machinery that they sometimes could not identify. Then one day in 1910 when Cataline stopped by, he gave the boy a beautiful colt named Paddy, which many years later Arthur Baker would describe as "just about the best horse in the country."[146]

Around this time Alex and Keith Peters, whose father was in charge of the Hudson's Bay Company post at Fraser Lake, were allowed to choose ponies from Cataline's pack train. Keith's choice was a docile animal, but the pinto pony Alex chose bucked, throwing him time and again, while Cataline stood there watching and laughing.

When one of the boys' older sisters had to be taken by sleigh over the Blackwater Trail to hospital in Quesnel, she insisted on taking her cat with her. "Somewhere along the way, the cat got away and they had to continue on without it. That spring Cataline paid the Peters family a visit. In his arms he carried the little girl's cat, which he had found along the trail."[147]

⊶⊷

54 year old

In April 1910, Pat Burns (1856–1937) was "just a lad" working at the Douglas Lake Ranch when he received a letter from his brother Bill in Kamloops telling him he had signed them both up for a cattle drive to Hazelton to bring "meat on the hoof" to the workers on the Grand Trunk Pacific Railway. Burns, who would create one of the world's largest integrated meat-packing empires and become one of the four founders of the Calgary Stampede, later recalled that expedition:

> We were to leave Ashcroft on April 20 for the Chilcotin to round up beef to start on the drive.... Our route followed the west side of the Fraser River.... At Quesnel we met Jean Cataline, the old packer, who had two pack trains loading up for the trip to Hazelton and north to the Ninth Cabin on the old Telegraph Trail. He had sixty mules and sixty horses in his train. From Cataline we got much information regarding the camping places along the trail, as there were only certain places where there was enough feed and room to night-herd the cattle, and where there was good water. Some of these spots were only three or four miles apart, others twelve to fifteen. We were always on the move by six o'clock in the morning, but sometime we would be in camp for the day by nine or ten.[149]

In the off-season, after settling his animals at Dog Creek, Cataline sometimes ventured to Vancouver, and in the winter of 1910, he was seen there by David Henry Hoy, a freighter and trapper from the Fort St. James district.

I met Cataline in Vancouver in 1910 in the old Strand Hotel, near the corner of Hastings and Granville streets. At that time he was getting to be a pretty old man, but he had come to the coast on a sort of holiday, he said, though I think he was there on business as well. He was wearing a dress suit and a cowboy hat, so that he would have been noticeable for that even apart from his remarkable figure. He was a fine-looking man, about medium height, and would have drawn attention anywhere. He was drinking rum neat, but it was not like our rum nowadays. It was the old Hudson's Bay Company rum that would strangle the ordinary man if he tried to drink it the way that Cataline was taking it down. He thought nothing of tossing a glass of it down neat. He had a peculiar way of drinking that caught the eye of anyone who was not used to seeing him but which got so that it was not noticed by those who were used to him. He never drained his glass but left a little in it, and this he spilled out on his fingers and rubbed it in his hair. If any checkako managed to muster up enough courage to ask him why he did this, the old man would answer in his great rolling voice that rum was a good thing for the stomach so it must be a good thing for the hair as well. He certainly had a fine head of hair, hanging down to his shoulders.[150]

A GIFT OF A COLT

Author Wiggs O'Neill (1882–1964), who had been the recipient of a colt from Cataline back in 1888, met him again in the Hazelton area.

> In 1910 I was purser on the steamer *Inlander* on the Skeena River. On our first trip on arriving in Hazelton I noticed a queer-looking old chap going up the street with long hair and flowing moustache and wearing moccasins. I inquired from someone who he was and was told he was Cataline, the famous packer. Right here the name registered.… I [had] first met him in 1888 on the Cariboo Road when I was just six years old. After my father died in Barkerville, my mother sent my oldest sister and me to live with our grandparents who had a ranch in the Bonaparte Valley on the Cariboo Road.
>
> One day Cataline was passing up the road with his big pack train of mules with his bell mare in the lead. He stopped up on the road and walked down the hill, leading a little black colt. I remember him well with his long black hair and big black moustache. He greeted my grandparents, Michael and Catherine Veasey, and told them his bell mare had given birth to a colt, and he found the colt too much trouble, so he wanted to leave it at the ranch as a present for the "leetle" boy. The little boy was me, so I became the owner of a real horse.

Now, twenty-two years later, O'Neill stood watching as Cataline kept on up the street and turned in at Black Jack McDonnell's saloon.

O'Neill followed him in and introduced himself, and over a drink, Cataline reminisced about O'Neill's grandparents as "my goot friends, goot Cath-licks too lak meself."[148]

Independent trader Martin Starret had moved into the Babine area in 1909, and many years later recalled an interesting meeting with Cataline.

> I think it was 1910 or '11.... It doesn't matter much which.... I was heading down to the Hud-son Bay store or warehouse in Hazelton, and I... fell in with Cataline. His train was gathered on the street. They took the entire street there. Oh, I suppose he had 60 head of mules and horses and probably six or seven packers there. There was a fellow tinkering with a horse there, shoeing a horse—one of these tall Mongolian guys—and [Cataline] says: "Here, Tom, you see that jenny over there? You take 'em all shoe off that mule. Take 'em all off."
>
> "You mean you want new shoes?"
>
> "No, leave 'em off. Four case of eggs go Babine. I put 'em one pack of eggs that mule." And then he turns to me and he said, "No shoe, he go out there and maybe 10 mile or 15 mile his feet get sore. He walk easy, just like a cat. Not break one egg." He made signs with his two hands. "He walk just like zee cat," he said. "Not break one egg going down the hill other side."[151]

Cataline's final contract took him along the Yukon Telegraph Trail, before he wintered his animals in the Bulkley Valley. Image I-57422 courtesy of the Royal BC Museum and Archives

But Cataline's stopovers in Hazelton were not all devoted to work in those days. H.M. Matthews, who clerked at the Hudson's Bay Company post, had the pleasure of his company on many occasions.

> We had at the post a building that was known as the stone cellar... a building built of cement and boulders about twenty by thirty feet [six by nine metres] in size, with walls a good twenty inches [fifty centimetres] thick. This was our liquor cellar. The Company, having a wholesale licence, were permitted to sell six bottles [per customer] of any one brand in stock. And we had some stock—barrels of rum, whiskeys of all kinds. Bottled wines—claret, port, sherry, champagne, plus all kinds of liqueurs, and the lowly beers and stouts....
>
> It was the custom then that, whenever a pack train leader or old customer arrived, to immediately trot him out to the stone cellar, offer him a glass and invite him to sample any of the barrels, of which there were many. In that way I served Cataline with many a tot of rum. And let me tell you, in those days Hudson's Bay rum was real powerful.
>
> The stories I have read about Cataline and the way he used to drink his rum are really out of this world. However, here is a true story about the event, and I have seen it done many and many a time. He would pour approximately four fingers of rum into an ordinary tumbler,

look at it, smell it, then with one swift motion down a good three fingers of it—without a choke or a catch of his breath. The remaining finger he would pour into his cupped hand, and rub it into his long hair, exclaiming vigorously at the same time: "Aghhhh—tres bon, tres bon!" and march out of the cellar. Just one drink—no more. The same ritual and routine every time."[152]

In the "Ashcroft Correspondence" column of the April 23, 1911, issue of Quesnel's *Cariboo Observer*, readers were told that:

Jean Caux Cataline, who has been in [Ashcroft] the past fortnight, left late this week for Dog Creek to organize his summer's pack train. As soon as he can do so, he will leave for Quesnel and other points on the government telegraph line to which he will pack the season's supplies.[153]

On June 3, the paper reported that:

Cataline's second pack train, part of which came up on the east side of the Fraser and part on the west side, arrived here on Tuesday last. About fifty horses were in the train, which was in charge of Cataline himself.[154]

And on August 24, 1911, the mining paper *The Ledge* announced admiringly that:

Joe Cataline, the government packer, has left Hazelton with 40,000 pounds [18,144 kilograms]

> of supplies for the telegraph offices between
> Hazelton and 9th cabin, a distance of 230 miles
> [370 kilometres). Joe is [73] years old and win-
> ters his pack train at Dog Creek after travelling
> 1,325 miles [2132 kilometres] each summer.[155]

In October, when Cataline and his crew returned to Hazelton after provisioning the telegraph line cabins, they discovered
that the right-of-way for the Grand Trunk Pacific Railway line had
been completed from there to the new port city of Prince Rupert.
This westernmost end of the line had been the most difficult and
expensive for the railway company because it involved building a
steel span bridge across the Skeena River and blasting three tunnels out of the walls of Kitselas Canyon. Although there was still a
gap of several hundred miles with the rails coming from the east,
during the following winter, workers laid the tracks from Prince
Rupert to Hazelton. From then on, goods that had travelled upriver to this point by sternwheeler would arrive by rail.

In the spring of 1912, Charlie Olds, an old-time trapper, railway
man and newspaperman, was on the road travelling from Vancouver to Fort Fraser, when he met Cataline and his pack train. In his
memoirs, Olds wrote:

> The next morning, at our camping site, I had
> my first meeting with the legendary government
> packer of early telegraph fame, Cataline.…
> This particular morning, one of the horses was
> missing, and the whole train was held up waiting
> for the wranglers to bring in the stray. The story
> goes that this drover never got off his horse ex-
> cept to sleep and then he just pulled the saddle

off the horse, and using it for a pillow, slept the few short hours of summer darkness…. This morning he was sitting ramrod straight in his saddle, his long hair reaching well below his shoulders.[157]

That spring, when Cataline and his pack train had set out from Dog Creek, their first stop had been the Ashcroft warehouses of the Harvey Bailey Company to pick up supplies destined for the Hudson's Bay Company posts north of Fort George. His crew included Dave McDaniels, William Vaughan, Serape Leon (the pack train's blacksmith), Pablo Tresierra, Skookum Joe, a "strapping Irishman" named Rufe Evans, Antwyne or Antoine Deschamps, who was the pack train's cook, and Ernest Thoreson, a Swede who was working for Cataline for the first time. Thoreson later recalled that

at that time [Cataline] was 83 years of age [he was actually 74 years in 1912], tall, powerfully built [and] at least 200 pounds in weight. He wore his hair long, down to his shoulders. His speech was broken. He talked slow but had a powerful voice…. He and Pablo when together always spoke Spanish. He did not drink liquor in camp or on the trail. Another thing I noticed [was] when he bought a pair of cowboy boots in Dog Creek, he put them on and stood in the horse trough for quite some time.[158]

By the beginning of August, Cataline and his pack train were in Hazelton, where they stopped at the Hudson's Bay Company warehouse to load up the provisions for the telegraph cabins before heading up the line. The *Omineca Miner* reported on August 3, 1912:

> Cataline, the veteran packer, arrived Tuesday from the Fort George country with sixty pack animals. He expects to leave today with supplies for the telegraph cabins on the Yukon Line, going as far as the Ninth Cabin.[159]

When the pack train was "somewhere north of Hazelton," Cataline sent Thoreson and two of the other men back to Hazelton with the animals that were no longer needed. Thoreson recalled:

> Next morning we had breakfast together for the last time. Cataline said as he shook my hand, "Don't go around kissing the wolf," and with a laugh said, "I may see you next spring." Cataline was a rough, tough man, but he was an honest man and never went back on his word. Well, we saddled up, and with 39 head of horses we took off down the trail. That was the last time I saw Cataline.[160]

The pack train continued north, cabin by cabin, until all of the remaining provisions had been distributed, and by the beginning of October, they were on their way south again. But somewhere near cabin #4, Antoine Deschamps died. In Hazelton, the *Omineca Miner* reported on October 26, 1912:

> A man named Deschamps, cook for Cataline, the packer, died on the trail near Fourth Cabin a few days ago.[161]

He was, according to the *Cariboo Observer*, one of Quesnel's "old timer residents."[162] He was probably simply worn out by the rigours of the trail, but his passing was a great loss to Cataline.

By mid-November, Cataline was back in Hazelton with the remainder of his pack train, but according to the *Omineca Miner*, instead of driving his animals all the way south to Dog Creek, he made an arrangement to winter them in the Bulkley Valley.[163]

Death of W.D. Jardine

On February 24, 1912, the *Omineca Miner* reported on the death of W.D. Jardine.

> The death occurred on Thursday morning of William Douglas Jardine, who has for some time occupied the position of accountant at the Hazelton Hotel. The deceased, who was well-known throughout the district, having been accountant for Jean Caux (Cataline) and later for the Omineca Hotel, had for years suffered from asthma. On Wednesday he was confined to his bed by what proved to be a final seizure. Though of quiet disposition, the deceased had many friends.... The funeral will be held this afternoon.[156]

RETIREMENT

Cataline retired from the trail in 1913. He had disposed of his second pack train during the winter and now sold his last sixty animals to his old friend George Biernes, who also took over his contract to provision telegraph cabins one to nine north of Hazelton and numbers one and two south of the town. The sale marked the end of Cataline's fifty-four-year packing career.

Through all his years of packing, Cataline had cared deeply about the welfare of his crew, especially when they were in financial need. Then, because he carried little cash and had no access to banks or stores on the trail, he would make use of the services of the Harvey Bailey Company as his personal bank.

One request sent on the letterhead of the General Store and Hotel at 150 Mile House and dated May 19, 1902, read:

> To Messrs Harvey Bailey:
>
> Please pay Charlie McGee wife $10 one month and charge to me goods from the store.
>
> Yours truly,
> Jean Caux

Charlie McGee was one of Cataline's pack train employees, and his wife was living in Ashcroft. The writer of the letter, acting on Caux's instructions, is unknown. Another note, written on a scrap of paper, is dated "Bonaparte, BC. April 19, 1904."

> To Harvey Bailey & Co, Ashcroft, BC.
>
> Please give the bearer Louis Haboose Indian of Bonaparte credit for fourteen dollars and charge to my account.
>
> Jean Caux

On May 7, 1906, writing on the stationery of the British Columbia Express Company, he sent a message to the Harvey Bailey Company, Ashcroft, BC, as follows:

> Gentlemen,
>
> Kindly give this Chinaman Ah Fook goods to the amount of $10 and charge to my account.
>
> Jean Caux

And on a plain piece of paper sent from Cache Creek on May 15, 1907:

> Dear Sir,
>
> Please give to Harry G. Ennis ten dollars $10.00 in cash and five dollars $5.00 in trade from the store and charge the same to my account.
>
> Yours respectfully,
> Jean Caux

In spite of making a great deal of money over the years, Cataline had been too generous with friends and crew and easily swindled, and by the time he had paid off his crew for the final time in 1913 and settled up his debts, he had little money left. Rumours later circulated that his money had been stolen by his former *cargador,* Ah Gun, but this was untrue. Gun was brought up in court in 1909, but it was the result of an ill-fated venture with a man named Jack Graham, with whom he had attempted to start a general store in Prince Rupert. Cataline faced his retirement more or less penniless because he had no pension or retirement fund set aside. In those days it was expected that family would take care of family, and if you had no family, your friends would rally around to support you. Sperry Cline, the constable in charge of the BC Provincial Police Force detachment in Hazelton, was one of those who came to Cataline's rescue. Cline recalled:

> This was before the days of easy government money, and as there was no old age pension and no welfare organization, it was largely up to the constable to look after the destitute in his district. In fact, everything that was too hot or unwholesome for other departments was added to his duties. [164]

Biernes, originally from Ontario, had come west to make his fortune in the Yukon gold rush but instead found work on the construction of the White Pass and Yukon Railway and the Yukon Telegraph. By 1906, he had assembled a train of mules and horses on a ranch at Mission Point across the Bulkley River from Hazelton, and as well as guiding hunting parties, he had entered the packing business by taking on the contract for the Grand Trunk Pacific Railway mail service. He was "a good-looking, cheerful, honest, tough, all-round outdoorsman.... With a fund of stories with which he regaled wealthy hunters as they sat around the campfire in the crisp evening air, he became deservedly popular among the hunting crowd."[165]

Biernes had built a small cabin on his ranch for Cataline, and it was described by another veteran of those packing years, Hugh McLean, as "100 feet [30 metres] from the house where George lived himself.... There was a stove, a little cook stove in it, and a bed. It was a roomy little place, too, and Cataline was stopping in that."

Although Cataline had seventy-five years of hard living behind him, he still had a number of good years left in him. But times were changing around him. The Grand Trunk Pacific Railway was completed in April 1914, improving access to goods and services in the north, and as trails became roads, many of the communities that had been serviced by his pack trains could now get supplies easily by horse and wagon—even by automobile. When war was declared in August 1914, many of the young men who had pioneered in the hinterlands of BC, especially those who had come from Britain, joined up to defend "the old country," leaving the farms and ranches they had pioneered in the Cariboo and the north to languish. In 1918, the federal government brought in prohibition, and Sperry Cline, who was still with the Hazelton detachment of the Provincial Police Force, found himself trying to "obtain even a meagre supply" of rum for Cataline.

> As tactfully as possible I approached different government departments, but I was told that there was no way of supplying him. Fortunately a high government official visited Hazelton. I explained Cataline's case and got a wink that a blind horse could have interpreted, and from then on managed to get him a limited supply.[166]

Cataline spent the winter of 1920 in Victoria's Dominion Hotel but soon returned to Hazelton. Image F-00016 courtesy the Royal BC Musem and Archives

Influenza swept the country in 1919. By 1920, Cataline was beginning to feel his age, and he decided that Hazelton winters were too hard and henceforth he would spend the winter months in Victoria. But it took just one winter in the Dominion Hotel in that city to make him decide he preferred the rigors of winter in the north to the traffic and noise of city life. He spent the remainder of his days in Hazelton.

During the last few months of his life, Sperry Cline saw him almost daily, and he later wrote:

He would sit and daydream for hours.... Towards the end many of his friends joined me in urging him to enter the hospital. He stoutly refused, honestly believing that a hospital was a place where people went to die. [Then one day in September 1922, Cataline took a bad turn and was put on a freight sleigh to be taken to hospital.] Soon after he was taken out into the cold, he revived, and when he realized where he was being taken, he rolled off the sleigh and started back to town. He informed us that he was "Noa ready to die nowa." A few weeks after this he submitted to entering the hospital where he died a few days later, probably wishing to play fairly with the hospital as he had with everyone else during his life. All he requested from the country that he had served so long and well was that he be given a Christian burial.

That then, was Cataline—or as much as I know of him. He was rough, rugged and picturesque as an individual, but more than that he was always completely fair, absolutely honest and utterly reliable. A man who didn't know what hardship was because that was his complete way of life.[167]

Jean Caux died on October 24, 1922, in the Hazelton hospital, and with him passed one of the last significant connections to the pioneer days of British Columbia. He left no will, and according to his friends, he didn't leave much else either—except fond memories and the rich legend of his life.

The *Victoria Daily Times,* October 27, 1922, reported on his death:

Jean Caux Takes Final Journey

Last winter, a bent venerable figure attracted the attention of everyone who had business at the Dominion Hotel. He looked as if the open air rather than the city streets had known him for many a year. He was Jean Caux, universally called "Cataline" throughout the north. Now a message from Prince Rupert announces his death.

He had reached the age of 92 [actually 84] and looked every year of it. Still he was able to care for himself. Something of his life story he told *The Times.* It was related in a halting mixture of English and French mixed with Chinook nouns and backwoods slang, and the French debased by the patois of the upland departments which slope from the Pyrénées, and here and there a Spanish word carried by the mountain villagers from the Catalonian side. He was born in a year of revolution, and as far as he could remember it was something to do with the third Napoleon that hastened his departure from the village of Gascony where he was born and grew to manhood. He crossed the ocean, gradually working west, and engaged in all manner of occupations until the gold rush of 1858 brought him on the flood tide to this province.

Opposite: Jean "Cataline" Caux died in Hazelton in 1922 at the age of 84. Image B-00699 courtesy of the Royal BC Museum and Archives

It was not, however, as a gold seeker that he earned a scanty livelihood, but as a packer and guide to the numerous survey parties which sought a reasonable route through the mountains to the Pacific Ocean.

More recently he had departed out of Hazelton, but as the years went on his strength failed, and he had eventually disposed of his mules and settled down. Then came last winter a desire to "come out" once more to see a relative here.

Cataline was buried in the Hazelton cemetery, and beside him lie four old friends: Jack Graham, packer; Joe Lyons, miner; Jim May, miner and prospector; and Ezra Evans, miner and one-time deputy mining recorder for Omineca.

Afterword

On November 15, 1905, Clemence Caux was married in a ceremony performed by Reverend J. Campbell, MA, PhD, by licence (as opposed to bans) at "The Manse," 277 Fort Street, Victoria. The groom was a thirty-one-year-old American teamster of Norwegian extraction named Anton (or Antoni) Heggen Lynn. It is obvious that Clemence was not the person who filled out the marriage certificate because the bride's place of birth is listed as Victoria and her parents as John and Mary Coax. And although Clemence had been baptised a Catholic and attended Catholic boarding schools for many years, the certificate gives the religion of both bride and groom as Presbyterian.

After the marriage, Clemence's son, Frederick, became known as Frederick Harris Lynn.

In September 1935, the federal government advised Clemence, who was living with her husband and son at 69 Crease Avenue in Victoria, that in 1910 her father had paid a security deposit of $690 to renew his annual provisioning contract for the Yukon Telegraph cabins between Hazelton and Telegraph Creek, and this money had not been returned to him after he carried out the contract. With accrued interest, the amount owing to him was now $948.32, a sizable amount of money in the middle of the Depression years. (At that time, a brand new luxury Ford convertible sedan could be bought for $750. The gas to fuel it was just 10¢ a gallon.)

In order to get this money, Clemence had to appeal to the Supreme Court of British Columbia to prove that her father, Jean Caux, had died a widower and intestate and that she was his natural and lawful daughter and his only next-of-kin. She did this on September 21, 1935, with the help of the esteemed lawyer Stuart Henderson, who had known and respected her father. In applying for and accepting this money, she was either unaware that her father had other children or was ignoring that fact, but it seems quite probable that he had never told her that she had half-siblings. They had, after all, taken another man's name.

Clemence's son, Frederick Harris Lynn, who became a bookkeeper for a paint manufacturer, never married and never left home. He died of pneumonia at St. Joseph's Hospital in Victoria on December 9, 1940. He was just thirty-nine and had suffered with diabetes mellitus most of his life.

Just three years later, Anton Lynn died; he was seventy years old. Clemence survived him by another ten years; she was seventy-three years old when she died as the result of a cerebral hemorrhage on February 14, 1953.

Amelia Paul, who was the mother of Cataline's first two children—Rhoda (Cecw'etkʷu), born around 1877, and William Benjamin (Kʷespaxan), born around 1878—also had a son, William Graham Jr. (Cinsq't), with settler William Graham, who later homesteaded in the Nicola Valley. With her third partner, a man named Harris, a telegraph operator from the Stikine, she had a second daughter, Clara (Kesutetkʷu), born about 1881. Amelia later married Paul Joseph York of Tikwalus, and they had a daughter,

Sarah (Wilktk^{w}u). Another daughter, Elizabeth York, died in early childhood.[168] Amelia Paul York had extensive cultural, social and genealogical knowledge of the people of Spuzzum, and she also became one of the foremost Nlaka'pamux basket weavers. As such, she was the subject of great interest to the Scottish ethnographer James Teit (1864–1922) and appears as subject #30 in *Coiled Basketry in British Columbia and Surrounding Regions*, which was published in 1928 with Herman K. Haeberlin and Helen H. Roberts as part of the 41st Annual Report of the Bureau of American Ethnology, 1919–1924.

Cataline and Amelia's daughter Rhoda (Cecw'etk^{w}u) had one son, Arthur Urquhart, who was well-respected in his community and later worked with a number of important anthropologists. Cataline and Amelia's son William Benjamin York married Lucy Palmer, and they had seven children—David, Albert, Annie, Thomas, Ethel, Harry (who died young) and Kathleen. David York married Edna Garcia, and their son, Kenneth, was raised by his York grandparents. Annie York (1904–91), like her grandmother Amelia, became very knowledgeable about the language and history of the Nlaka'pamux people. She worked with Richard Daly and Chris Arnett on *They Write Their Dreams on the Rock Forever: Rock Writings in the Stein Valley of British Columbia* (published in 1993) and with Andrea Laforet on *Spuzzum: Fraser Canyon Histories, 1908–1939* (published in 1998).

Amelia's daughter Clara (Kesutetk^{w}u) (1881–1974) married Frank Clare, and they had five children. One of Clara's great-granddaughters, Irene Bjerky, has—like Annie York—undertaken much research into the family's history.

Endnotes

○══╼○

The Fraser River Gold Rush

1. Interview with Judge Henry Castillou, Imbert Orchard, "People in Landscape: Fraser River Country," Imbert Orchard fonds, accession no. 2440, tape 1, track 1, BC Archives (hereafter BCA).

2. Ancestry.com, *New York, Passenger Lists, 1820–1957* (online database). Ancestry.com Operations, Inc., Provo, UT, 2010. Original data: *Passenger Lists of Vessels Arriving at New York, New York, 1820–1897,* microfilm publication M237, 675 rolls, NAI: 6256867. Records of the US Customs Service, record group 36, National Archives at Washington, DC.

3. *1901* Census, *Lillooet (East/est), Yale & Cariboo, British Columbia, 1,* family No. *14.* Retrieved from Ancestry.com, *1901 Census of Canada* (online database). Ancestry.com Operations Inc., Provo, UT, 2006. Original data: Library and Archives Canada, *Census of Canada, 1901,* series RG31-C-1, microfilm reels T-6428 to T-6556, Statistics Canada fonds, Library and Archives Canada, 2004, www.bac-lac.gc.ca/eng/census/1901/Pages/about-census.aspxl.

4. *Victoria Daily Times,* October 27, 1922.

5. Noel Duclos, *Packers, Pans and Paydirt* (Quesnel, BC: Arthur Duclos, 1995), 64–65.

6.   George Ogston, "Early Days in the Nechako Valley," in *Pioneer Days in British Columbia*, vol. 4, Art Downs, ed. (Surrey, BC: Heritage House, 1979), 103.

7.   Interview with Judge Henry Castillou, Orchard, "People in Landscape."

8.   Reminiscences of William Francis Manson, Indian Constable at Stoney Creek, October 2, 1929, 2/18, E E M311, BCA.

9.   Reminiscences of Mrs. August Baker (born Suzie Elmore) of Quesnel, October 11, 1929, 8/12, E C B172.2, BCA.

10. C.B. (Bill) Bailey, "Cataline—Cariboo Packer," *Vancouver Daily Province*, January 25, 1947.

11. Interview with Judge Henry Castillou, Orchard, "People in Landscape."

12. Notes from a conversation with James Nathaniel Jerome Brown, carpenter, as told to Robert Hartley, Vancouver, July 7, 1930, 9/10, E C B81.3, BCA.

13. Jean Barman, *The West Beyond the West: A History of British Columbia* (Toronto: University of Toronto Press, 1991), 62.

14. Lorraine Harris, *The Fraser Canyon: From Cariboo Road to Super Highway* (Surrey, BC: Hancock House, 1984), 7.

15. Peter Charles, *At the '47 Mile: A History of the Village of Clinton* (Victoria: Orca Books, 1990), 36.

16. Harris, *The Fraser Canyon*, 6–7.

17. Mike Cleven, *The Trail of 1858: British Columbia's Gold Rush Past*, cayoosh.net, 55–56.

18. Whannell to Douglas, December 31, 1858, quoted in Donald J. Hauka, *McGowan's War* (Vancouver: New Star Books, 2003), 145.

19. Sperry Cline, "Cataline," BCA, E E C61, Burnaby, BC, March 1959, unpublished manuscript, 4–5.

20. Don Logan, *Dog Creek: 100 Years* (Victoria: Trafford Publishing, 2007), 92.

21. Roderick J. Barman, "Packing in British Columbia: Transport on a Resource Frontier," *Journal of Transportation History* 21, no. 2: 145–46.

22. Interview with Alan Benson, Imbert Orchard, "People in Landscape: Fraser River Country," Imbert Orchard fonds, accession no. 2440, tape 1, track 1, BCA.

23. Frank Sylvester, address to the Board of Trade in Victoria, circa 1907–08, quoted in Lloyd Jeck, *British Columbia Trails Heading North* (Clearwater, BC: Maieck Publishing, 2011), 170–78.

THE CARIBOO GOLD RUSH

24. BCARS, G -90 -261, uncatalogued treasury records, Government Record Book, Lytton City. Note by Chris Hanna.

25. Marie Elliott, "The Gold Rush Pack Trail of 1861," *BC Historical News* (Summer 2000): 19.

26. Lorna Townsend, "The Dregs of Society," unpublished article, 2008.

27. Jo Lindley, *Three Years in Cariboo: Being the Experience and Observations of a Packer, What I Saw and Know of the Country; Its Traveled Routes, Distances, Villages, Mines, Trade and Prospects with Distances, Notes and Facts* (San Francisco: A. Rosenfeld, 1862), 11–12.

28. Toll and Duty Record Book, September 1, 1862, and December 17, 1864, BCA, add. mss. 2013.

29. R. Barman, "Packing in British Columbia," 143–44.

30. R. Barman, 147.

31. S.G. Hathaway, BCA, manuscript call no. E B H28A.

32. J. Barman, *The West Beyond the West*, 67–68.

33. R. Barman, "Packing in British Columbia," 156.

34. R. Barman, 149–50.

35. Hilary Place, *Dog Creek: A Place in the Cariboo* (Surrey, BC: Heritage House, 1999), 10.

36. Mark Sweeten Wade, *The Cariboo Road* (Victoria, BC: Haunted Bookshop, 1979).

37. Branwen Patenaude, *Trails to Gold*, vol. 1 (Victoria: Horsdal & Schubart, 1995), 84.

38. Logan, *Dog Creek*, 11–12.

THE CARIBOO WAGON ROAD

39. J.T. Pidwell, colonial correspondence, 1869, cited in Trelle Morrow, *Cataline: Packer Extraordinaire* (Prince George, BC: Talisman Productions, 2013), 36.

40. *Cariboo Sentinel* (Barkerville, BC), September 4, 1869.

41. Pidwell, colonial correspondence, cited in Morrow, 36.

42. *Cariboo Sentinel*, August 20, 1870.

43. *Cariboo Sentinel*, August 19, 1871.

44. Interview with Martin Starret, Imbert Orchard, "People in Landscape: Fraser River Country," Imbert Orchard fonds, accession no. 2440, tape 1, track 1, BCA.

45. L.G. Temple, "Cataline: The King of Packers," in *The Shoulder Strap: Policing the West*, 23rd ed. (Vancouver: Department of the Attorney General, British Columbia Police, 1951), 71.

46. Interview with Judge Henry Castillou, Orchard, "People in Landscape."

47. Cecille Carroll, cited in *Wild and Free* by Frank Cooke as told to Jack Boudreau (Halfmoon Bay, BC: Caitlin Press, 2002), 23.

48. Ogston, "Early Days in the Nechako Valley," 102–07.

49. Pat Foster, *Historic Ashcroft for the Strong Eye Only* (Kamloops, BC: Plateau Press, 1999), 16–17.

50. Temple, "Cataline: The King of Packers," 72.

51. Cline, "Cataline," 8–9.

52. Cline, 8–9.

53 "French Relief Fund: General Compte Rendu," *British Colonist* (Victoria), August 31, 1871.

THE OMINECA GOLD RUSH OF 1869

54. R. Barman, "Packing in British Columbia," 155.

55. Jane Stevenson, *A Trail of Two Telegraphs and Other Historic Tales of the Bulkley Valley and Beyond* (Halfmoon Bay, BC: Caitlin Press, 2013), 13.

56. Lizette Hall, *The Carrier, My People* (Cloverdale, BC: Friesen Printers, 1992), 74.

57. Email correspondence with Joyce Helweg, plus a scan of a receipt. March 6, 2013.

58. *Mainland Guardian* (New Westminster), December 9, 1871.

59. General Sir William Francis Butler, *The Wild Northland: Being the Story of a Winter Journey, with Dog, across Northern North America* (Toronto: The Courier Press, 1911), 297.

60. Butler, 297.

CATALINE AND THE LAW

61. *Cariboo Sentinel,* June 6, 1865.

62. *Cariboo Sentinel,* December 2, 1871.

63. *Cariboo Sentinel,* December 2, 1871.

64. *Cariboo Sentinel,* December 2, 1871.

65. *Cariboo Sentinel,* December 8, 1871.

66. Cline, "Cataline," 2–5.

THE STIKINE AND CASSIAR GOLD RUSHES

67. "Yukon Telegraph: Chronology," in "An Explorer's Guide to the North," quoting from Department of Public Works records (Archival #RG11), Explore North, www.explorenorth.com.

68. *Daily British Colonist,* March 2, 1876.

69. *Daily British Colonist,* November 2, 1876, 3.

FAMILY TIES

70. Jennifer Pecho, Archivist, Records Manager, and Privacy Coordinator, Catholic Archdiocese of Vancouver, email correspondence, November 8, 2010.

71. Andrea Laforet and Annie York, *Spuzzum: Fraser Canyon Histories, 1808–1939* (Vancouver: UBC Press, 1998), 25.

72. Laforet and York, 142.

73. Carey Pallister, Assistant Archivist, Sisters of St. Ann, Victoria, BC, e-correspondence.

74. Register books, Sisters of Saint Ann Archives, Victoria, BC.

75. *Daily British Colonist*, April 12, 1882.

The Canadian Pacific Railway

76. *Inland Sentinel* (Yale), May 4, 1882.

77. *Inland Sentinel* (Yale), May 11, 1882.

78. R. Barman, "Packing in British Columbia," 144.

79. Interview with Tom Carolan, Imbert Orchard, "People in Landscape: Fraser River Country," Imbert Orchard fonds, accession no. 2440, tape 1, track 1, BCA.

80. Ogston, "Early Days in the Nechako Valley," 103.

81. Reminiscences of William Francis Manson, Indian Constable at Stoney Creek, October 2, 1929, 10, unpublished manuscript, BCA, E E M311.

82. Foster, *Historic Ashcroft*, 15.

83. Temple, "Cataline: The King of Packers," 72.

84. Foster, *Historic Ashcroft*, 14–15.

85. C.B. (Bill) Bailey, "Cataline—Cariboo Packer," *Vancouver Daily Province,* January 25, 1947.

86. Lily Chow, *Chasing Their Dreams: Chinese Settlement in the Northwest Region of British Columbia* (Halfmoon Bay, BC: Caitlin Press, 2000), xvii.

87. Foster, *Historic Ashcroft*, 7.

88. Comments by Virginia Bell, granddaughter of William Bailey, from a caption attached to a photograph on Flickr that is no longer available.

89. Place, *Dog Creek*, 11–12.

90. Place, *Dog Creek*, 11.

91. Temple, "Cataline: The King of Packers," 72.

92. Interview with Judge Henry Castillou, Orchard, "People in Landscape."

93. Interview with Judge Henry Castillou.

94. "Whisky Cases," *British Colonist*, July 24, 1860.

95. Interview with Judge Henry Castillou.

96. Foster, *Historic Ashcroft*, 9.

97. Peg Deeder of François Lake to Miss M. Wolfenden, June 18, 1945, BCA; this letter was discovered in a binder at the Quesnel Museum.

98. Cline, "Cataline," *BC Outdoors* 26 (November–December 1970): 49.

THE YUKON FIELD FORCE

99. Louis LeBourdais, Louis LeBourdais Collection, vol. 9, file 19: Cataline file, unpublished manuscript, November 22, 1934, 2–3, BCA, add. ms. 676.

100. Sperry Cline, BCA, E E C61, Cataline, Burnaby, BC, March 1959, unpublished manuscript, 5–7.

101. Bill Miller, *Wires in the Wilderness: The Story of the Yukon Telegraph* (Victoria: Heritage House, 2004), 82.

102. Brereton Greenhous, "Faith Fenton's & Georgia Powell's Despatches," in *Guarding the Goldfields: The Story of the Yukon Field Force* (Toronto: Dundurn Press, 1987), 115–16.

103. Greenhous, 119.

104. Brereton Greenhous, ed., "Edward Lester's Diaries," in *Guarding the Goldfields: The Story of the Yukon Field Force*, (Toronto: Dundurn Press, 1987), 54.

105. Greenhous, 56–57.

106. Greenhous, 87.

107. Greenhous, 103–04.

108. Cline, "Cataline," 5–7.

109. Hudson's Bay Company, Quesnelle, BC, to R.H. Hall, Victoria, May 15, 1899, Victoria correspondence outward, Cariboo District (Quesnel), 1899–1908, B226, b, 53.2/M, Hudson's Bay Company Archives held in the Archives of Manitoba, Winnipeg (hereafter HBC Archives).

110. Hudson's Bay Company, anonymous, Bulkley Valley Ranch (revised 1983), HBC Archives.

111. Hudson's Bay Company, Hall, Victoria, to Boyd, Quesnel, January 21, 1899, Victoria correspondence outward, Cariboo District (Quesnel), 1898–1900, B 226 b, 53.2/N, file 1 Interior Freighting, HBC Archives.

112. Hudson's Bay Company, McNabb, Stuart's Lake, to Hall, Victoria, November 4, 1898, Victoria correspondence outward, Cariboo District (Quesnel), 1898–1900, B226, b, 53.2/N, file 1, Interior Freighting, HBC Archives.

113. Hudson's Bay Company, Hall, Victoria, to Boyd, Quesnel, March 25, 1899, Victoria correspondence outward, Cariboo District (Quesnel), 1898–1900, B226, b, 53.2/N, file 1, Interior Freighting, HBC Archives.

114. Hudson's Bay Company, Quesnelle, BC, to R.H. Hall, Esq., Victoria, May 15, 1899, Victoria correspondence outward, Cariboo District (Quesnel), 1899–1908, B226, b, 53.2/M, HBC Archives.

115. Hudson's Bay Company, Hall, Victoria, to Boyda, Quesnelle, November 9, 1899, Victoria correspondence outward, Cariboo District (Quesnel), 1898–1900, B 226 b, 53.2/N, file 1, Interior Freighting, HBC Archives.

116. Hudson's Bay Company, Victoria correspondence outward, Cariboo District (Quesnel), 1898–1900, B 226 b, 53.2/N, file 1, Interior Freighting, HBC Archives.

117. Hudson's Bay Company, Victoria correspondence outward, Cariboo District (Quesnel), f, Interior Freighting, HBC Archives.

THE YUKON TELEGRAPH LINE

118. "Yukon Telegraph: Chronology," www.explorenorth.com.

119. Guy Lawrence, letter to the editor, *British Columbia Digest* 17 (January–February 1962): 45.

120. Alice Northcott Earley, "Alice Northcott Recalls Early Days: Reminiscences of Alice Earley," *Quesnel Cariboo Observer,* March 24, 1976.

121. Louis LeBourdais, Cataline File, unpublished manuscript, 1, BCA.

122. Lawrence, letter to the editor, 46.

123. "The Dominion Telegraph," www.telegraphtrail.org/history/section25.htm. This website, originally run by Dwight Dodge, is no longer active. Dwight Dodge ran the Telegraph Trail Preservation Society in Quesnel until 2006 and remained interested in the trail until his death in 2016.

124. "Yukon Telegraph: Chronology," www.explorenorth.com.

125. Hudson's Bay Company, Bulkley Valley Ranch (Revised 1983), note 8, HBC Archives.

126. Hudson's Bay Company, James Thompson, Victoria, to A.C. McNabb, Hazelton, January 23, 1902, MF 1214, HBC Archives.

127. Hudson's Bay Company, W. Bailey, Ashcroft, to James Thompson, Victoria, January 4, 1902, Victoria correspondence outward, Cariboo District (Quesnel), 1901–02, section B, class 226, subdivision b, piece 53.2/N, file 2, Interior Freighting, HBC Archives.

128. Bailey to Thomson, HBC correspondence, February 5, 1902.

129. Thompson to Bailey, HBC correspondence, February 8, 1902.

130. Bailey to Thompson, HBC correspondence, February 13, 1902.

131. Clemence G. Caux to "Mr. Jean Caux, Ashcroft," Victoria, February 18, 1902, Archival Holdings, Quesnel Museum.

132. Jean Caux to Thompson, manager, Hudson's Bay Company, Victoria, January 3, 1904, Victoria correspondence outward, Cariboo District (Quesnel), 1904–05, section B, class 226, subdivision b, piece 53.2/N, file 3, Interior Freighting, HBC Archives.

133. Hudson's Bay Company, James Thompson, Victoria, to Lockyer, Vancouver, January 9, 1904, Victoria correspondence

outward, Cariboo District (Quesnel), 1904–05, section B, class 226, subdivison b, piece 53.2/N, file 3, Interior Freighting, HBC Archives.

134. Hudson's Bay Company, Victoria correspondence outward, Cariboo District (Quesnel), 1904–05, section B, class 226, subdivison b, piece 53.2/N, file 3, Interior Freighting, HBC Archives.

135. James Thompson, Victoria, to J.C. Boyd, Hazelton, June 27, 1907, MF 1214, Hudson's Bay Company Archives.

136. Louis LeBourdais, "Cataline: Most Famous of all Old Cariboo's Pack-train Bosses," *Vancouver Sunday Province*, September 27, 1925.

137. Louis LeBourdais, "The Check That Told Stories," *Vancouver Sunday Province*, April 2, 1933.

138. Ogston, "Early Days in the Nechako Valley," 103.

THE FINAL ADVENTURE

139. Ogston, 103; see also Logan, *Dog Creek*, 90.

140. Lenore Rudland, *Fort Fraser (Where the Hell Is That?)*, (Sechelt, BC: Eric and Lenore Rudland, 1988), 32.

141. *Omineca Herald* (Hazelton, BC), February 29, 1929.

142. Frank Cooke, as told to Boudreau, *Wild And Free*, 25–26.

143. Cecille Carroll, "Cataline," *True West Magazine* (April 1993), 28–32, 37.

144. *Ashcroft Journal*, May 1, 1909.

145. Chantall Ryane, Archives Technician, Collections, Research and Access, Royal BC Museum, Victoria, email correspondence, August 14, 2012.

146. Ginny Dunn, excerpt from an article about Art Baker, *Quesnel Cariboo Observer*, August 11, 1971, 9.

147. *Deep Roots and Greener Valleys*, 2nd printing (Fraser Lake, BC: Fraser Lake & District Historical Society, 1987), 15.

148. Wiggs O'Neill, "Memories of a Famous Packer," *Kitimat Northern Sentinel*, September 27, 1962.

149. Wes Jasper, "Twelve Thousand Head North," *Omineca Herald* (Terrace), reprinted in *Pioneer Legacy: Chronicles of the Lower Skeena River*, vol. 2, compiled by Norma V. Bennett for the Dr. R.E.M. Lee Hospital Foundation (Terrace, BC: 2000), 196.

150. David Henry Hoy, reminiscences, interviewed in Prince George, October 8, 1929, E E H85 11, unpublished transcript, 9.

151. Interview with Martin Starret, Orchard, "People in Landscape."

152. H.M. Matthews, *Cariboo Digest*, date unknown, Quesnel Museum file on Cataline.

153. *Cariboo Observer* (Quesnel, BC), April 23, 1911.

154. *Cariboo Observer*, June 3, 1911.

155. *The Ledge* (Greenwood, BC), BC mining camp newspaper, August 24, 1911.

156. *Omineca Miner* (Hazelton, BC), February 24, 1912.

157. Charlie Olds, "Attracted to Nechako Valley," from an unpublished manuscript entitled "Looking Back" included in Audrey Smedley L'Heroux, ed., *From Trail to Rail: Settlement Begins 1905–1915* (Vanderhoof, BC: Northern BC Book Publishing, 1989), 46.

158. Logan, *Dog Creek*, 90.

159. *Omineca Miner*, August 3, 1912.

160. Logan, *Dog Creek*, 91.

161. *Omineca Miner*, October 26, 1912.

162. *Cariboo Observer* , November 23, 1912.

163. *Omineca Miner*, November 16, 1912.

RETIREMENT

164. Cline, "Cataline," 2–5.

165. David Ricardo Williams, *Simon Peter Gunanoot: Trapline Outlaw* (Victoria: Sono Nis Press, 1982), 131–32.

166. Cline, "Cataline," 2–5.

167. Cline, 12–13.

AFTERWORD

168. Andrea Laforet and Annie York, *Spuzzum*, 30–31.

ABOUT THE AUTHORS

SUSAN SMITH-JOSEPHY is a writer, researcher and genealogist. She trained as a journalist at Langara College and has worked for a number of small-town newspapers in BC. She has a degree in History from SFU, and is passionate about BC history. She lives in Quesnel, BC. Her first book *Lillian Alling: The Journey Home* was published by Caitlin Press in 2011.

IRENE BJERKY, C'EYXKN's interest in Jean Caux (Cataline) began many years ago, when she started researching her genealogical connection to him. Irene is a member of the Yale First Nation, and her great-great-grandmother was Amelia York, C'eyxkn, a well-known basketmaker and mother to two of Cataline's children. Irene is a boilermaker, and a former commercial fisher, and she is interested in her family's and community's history. She makes her home in Yale, BC.